X

BREXIT: Directions for Britain Outside the EU

BREXIT: DIRECTIONS FOR BRITAIN OUTSIDE THE EU

RALPH BUCKLE

TIM HEWISH

JOHN C. HULSMAN

IAIN MANSFIELD

ROBERT OULDS

Institute of
Economic Affairs

First published in Great Britain in 2015 by
The Institute of Economic Affairs
2 Lord North Street
Westminster
London SW1P 3LB
in association with London Publishing Partnership Ltd
www.londonpublishingpartnership.co.uk

The mission of the Institute of Economic Affairs is to improve understanding of the fundamental institutions of a free society by analysing and expounding the role of markets in solving economic and social problems.

A CIP catalogue record for this book is available from the British Library.

ISBN 978-0-255-36681-6

Many IEA publications are translated into languages other than English or are reprinted. Permission to translate or to reprint should be sought from the Director General at the address above.

Typeset in Kepler by T&T Productions Ltd
www.tandtproductions.com

Printed and bound in Great Britain by Page Bros

CONTENTS

The authors   vii
Foreword   ix
Acknowledgement   xii
Editorial note   xiii
List of tables, figures and boxes   xiv

1   A blueprint for Britain: openness not isolation   1
     Iain Mansfield

     Framing the endeavour   1
     External negotiations   2
     Internal preparations   20
     Outcomes   37
     Conclusion   42
     Appendix A: Analysis of trade policy options   45
     Appendix B: Analysis of outcomes   49
     References   57

**2   Britain's post-EU future and the development of
     EFTA plus   59**
     Robert Oulds

     Introduction   59
     The EU and 'free' trade   60
     Aims and objectives: the desired outcomes of negotiations
        with the EU   62
     Negotiations under the Article 50: the EU's prescribed
        method of withdrawal   66
     EU law post-Brexit   70
     British post-Brexit influence in the EU   72
     Post-EU trade and migration policy   74

The process of rejoining EFTA   98
Reforming the EEA and EFTA: re-establishing the original
  purpose of the EEA   99
Conclusion   104
Appendix A. The alternatives   106
Appendix B. Additional benefits of EFTA/EEA membership   108
Appendix C. Problems with the Swiss option   109
References   110

**3   Old links, new ties – global free trade through the
    Anglosphere and Commonwealth   112**
Ralph Buckle and Tim Hewish

Introduction   112
Why the Commonwealth and Anglosphere nations?   113
Current economic trends   119
The Internet   122
Should Britain join an enlarged NAFTA?   124
EFTA – a possible stopgap?   125
A trade deal down under: Australia and New Zealand   127
Conclusion   142
References   143

**4   Reviving the age of Drake: how a Global Free-
    Trade Alliance (GFTA) can transform the UK   146**
John C. Hulsman

Introduction: the benefits of thinking big   146
The Global Free-Trade Alliance (GFTA)   148
GFTA criteria in detail   151
Initial GFTA membership and the updated cohort   153
The advantages of living in Drake's world   156
Conclusion: deciphering the riddle of Drake's prayer   159
References   159

About the IEA   162

THE AUTHORS

Ralph Buckle

Ralph Buckle is a director and co-founder of the Commonwealth Exchange. He has considerable political, campaigning and event management experience, having worked for think tanks, politicians, public affairs agencies and political communication specialists. He has a BA in Politics, Philosophy and Economics (PPE) from the University of York.

Tim Hewish

Tim Hewish is a director and co-founder of the Commonwealth Exchange. He has a masters in Imperial and Commonwealth History and a strong knowledge of the Commonwealth as author of *Common-Trade, Common-Growth, Common-Wealth*.

Dr John C. Hulsman

Dr John C. Hulsman is the president and co-founder of John C. Hulsman Enterprises (www.john-hulsman.com), a global political risk consulting firm. An eminent foreign policy expert, John is a senior columnist on foreign affairs for *City AM* and also writes regularly for the Aspen Institute of Italy and *Limes*, the premier Italian foreign affairs journal. A veteran of think tanks in Europe and America, Hulsman is a life member of the Council on Foreign Relations. Author or co-author of ten books, Hulsman has also given 1,470 interviews, written over 330 articles and delivered more than 450 speeches on foreign policy around the world.

Iain Mansfield

Iain Mansfield is the Director of Trade and Investment at the UK's embassy in the Philippines and has previously worked for the Department of Business, Innovation and Skills. He lives with his wife, Sarah, who teaches at the British School, Manila. Iain is also the author of the novel, *Imperial Visions*, and has a masters in Natural Sciences from the University of Cambridge.

Robert Oulds

Robert Oulds, MA, FRSA, is the longstanding Director of the Bruges Group, the respected think tank which for the last 20 years has been at the forefront of the debate about the UK's relationship with the EU and the wider world. He is the author of *Everything You Wanted to Know about the EU but Were Afraid to Ask*. Robert Oulds is also the author of *Montgomery and the First War on Terror*. The book details a little-known period of Monty's career. Bernard Law Montgomery, later Field Marshal Viscount Montgomery of Alamein, faced guerrilla forces in Ireland in the early 1920s and Palestine on the eve of World War II. That book explores the lessons of Monty's victories in those conflicts and how they should be applied today in the modern war on terror.

FOREWORD

During 2013–14, the IEA ran a competition to find the best blue-print for Britain outside the EU, with the objective of securing a free and prosperous economy should we leave.

The IEA does not have a position on whether Britain should leave the EU. However, it is part of our educational mission to promote a wider understanding of the importance of a free economy and the institutions that are necessary for a free economy. We therefore regarded it as important to promote debate on the best way to achieve this in the event of the British people choosing to leave the EU: that was the main purpose of the competition.

To provide a longer-lasting contribution to this debate, the IEA decided to publish this monograph examining the various options using, in the main, entries to the Brexit competition. There was a wide range of possible approaches suggested by entrants to that competition. Some proposed that Britain should promote free trade and openness through the unilateral removal of trade and other barriers to economic activity; others proposed maintaining formal relationships with European countries through the European Free Trade Association and/or the European Economic Area; still other entrants took the view that Britain should seek to form economic and political alliances and partnerships with countries outside Europe – for example with the Commonwealth or the Anglosphere – normally with a view to that being a gateway to free trade with as much of the world as would be willing.

Inevitably, Foreign Office diplomat Iain Mansfield, who was the winner, received most of the publicity at the end of the competition.

However, in understanding how Britain can be free and prosperous in the event that we leave the EU, it is worthwhile considering a range of other approaches to Brexit. It is only through determining the best destiny for Britain outside the EU that the correct decision will be taken about whether to leave the EU and, if so, how. This monograph therefore brings together Iain Mansfield's submission with edited versions of two other entries. One of those, by Robert Oulds, proposes that the UK remains a member of the European Economic Area and rejoins the European Free Trade Association; another, by Ralph Buckle and Tim Hewish, proposes that Britain pursues free trade through the route of the Commonwealth and the Anglosphere. The final contribution to this monograph, by John Hulsman, was not an entry to the competition but re-examines and brings up to date an approach to promoting free trade first proposed in his IEA monograph published in 2001, *The World Turned Rightside Up*. This involved the development of a global free-trade association.

Overall, this monograph is an important contribution to the debate about how Britain should leave the EU should it choose to do so. It distils clearly the different options and the advantages and disadvantages of alternative approaches with reference to the objective of promoting a free and prosperous economy. Clearly the authors have different views about how to achieve the same objective. It is hoped that, by presenting those different views in this volume, the debate will move beyond 'Britain – in or out?' to a debate about something just as important: 'Should Britain leave, how should it leave?'

The views expressed in this monograph are, as in all IEA publications, those of the author and not those of the Institute (which has no corporate view), its managing trustees, Academic Advisory Council members or senior staff. With some exceptions, such as with the publication of lectures, all IEA monographs are blind peer-reviewed by at least two academics or researchers who are experts in the field. The content of this monograph was not peer reviewed. However, all but one of the chapters was reviewed by members of the Brexit judging panel (see acknowledgement).

PHILIP BOOTH
Editorial and Programme Director
Institute of Economic Affairs
Professor of Insurance and Risk Management
Cass Business School, City University, London
January 2015

ACKNOWLEDGEMENT

The IEA would like to thank the judging panel for the Brexit competition: Rt. Hon. Lord Lawson of Blaby (Chairman); Professor Philip Booth (Facilitator); Roger Bootle; Tim Frost; Ruth Lea; Dr David Starkey; Gisela Stuart MP; Professor Martin Ricketts; Dr Stephen Davies and Robert Craig (advisor to the judges). Roger Bootle and Ruth Lea stood down as formal members of the panel in the later stages to avoid possible conflicts of interests.

EDITORIAL NOTE

The IEA monograph and book series are being reorganised to better reflect the nature of the different types of publications we produce. In the future, there will be two series, Hobart Paperbacks and Readings in Political Economy. The former series will include more directly policy-oriented publications and longer studies of a particular area of economics. Effectively, this series will be a merger of the former Hobart Papers, Hobart Paperbacks and Research Monographs. The first Hobart Paperback in the new format will therefore take the number following that of the last Hobart Paper. Readings in Political Economy will include primers, lectures and more philosophical works.

TABLES, FIGURES AND BOXES

Table 1   Comparative positions of Norway, Switzerland and
          Turkey and proposed UK position after exit   4
Table 2   Free trade agreements of Switzerland, Norway, New
          Zealand and the EU with non-EU G20 countries   8
Table 3   The UK's top ten non-EU, non-EFTA export
          destinations (2012)   10
Table 4   Initial priority order for non-EU, non-EFTA FTA
          negotiations   11
Table 5   Likely topics for negotiation in a UK exit agreement   19
Table 6   Impact on GDP of the best-case, most likely and
          worst-case scenarios   40
Table 7   UK exports (goods and services) 2002–12 (£bn)   47
Table 8   UK trade export growth (goods and services),
          2002–12   48
Table 9   FTA priority conclusions   50
Table 10 Cost of UK exit as calculated by comparison with the
          TTIP   51
Table 11 UK benefit or loss from selected FTAs   53
Table 12 Impact on GDP of the best-case, most likely and
          worst-case scenarios   56
Table 13 Foreign direct investment flows per capita per year
          (US $)   80
Table 14 World Bank's Ease of Doing Business rankings   121
Table 15 World Bank's 'Starting a Business' rankings   121
Table 16 World Bank's 'protecting investors' rankings   121
Table 17 The Corruption Perception Index   122

Figure 1   Percentage of UK exports to the EU and ROW   9
Figure 2   How does the UK spend the money it receives from
           the EU?   32
Figure 3   UK trade balance with EU in goods and in services   63
Figure 4   FDI in Iceland, Switzerland, Norway in comparison
           with the UK (1983–2012), Central Bank of Iceland
           (1989–2012)   80
Figure 5   Commonwealth and Europe share of real world GDP
           (PPP, $bn) 1970–2013   120

Box 1   Article 50 of the Lisbon Treaty   2
Box 2   What is the Single Market?   6
Box 3   Regulations and directives   22
Box 4   Super-affirmative procedure   24
Box 5   Excerpt from a summary of EU driving regulations
           for vehicles over 3.5 tonnes   25
Box 6   New Zealand   123

1 A BLUEPRINT FOR BRITAIN: OPENNESS NOT ISOLATION[1,2]

Iain Mansfield

FRAMING THE ENDEAVOUR

An 'out' vote has occurred and the government has triggered Article 50 of the Lisbon Treaty. Under the terms of the Treaty (see Box 1), the UK will cease to be a member of the EU two years after that date. To steady the markets, the UK government should declare as soon as possible that it intends to observe the two-year period and not negotiate for an earlier date. This will allow as much time as possible for the many necessary preparations and remove a potential distraction from the many other and more complex items that will need to be negotiated.

This paper assumes that, in the case of an 'out' vote, the government of the day, regardless of party, would respect the position of the British populace in demanding a substantive change in the UK's relationship with the EU and would therefore not seek to essentially duplicate the current status via a series of bilateral treaties. Equally, it assumes that the purpose of leaving the EU

---

1   *Disclaimer.* This paper is written in a personal capacity and does not represent the formal position of the British Embassy Manila, Foreign and Commonwealth Office or Her Majesty's Government.

2   *Acknowledgements.* Grateful thanks for thoughts, suggestions and comments go to the following people: Miranda Dawkins; Guy Digby; Michael Gasiorek; Peter Holmes; Owen Jones; James Matthews; Susie Roques; Julia Shvets; David Smy; Alex Wright. The opinions and conclusions expressed in this paper, as well as any errors, remain fully the responsibility of the author.

Box 1   Article 50 of the Lisbon Treaty[1]

Under Article 50, to leave the EU a member state need simply notify the European Council of its intent. The EU treaties shall cease to apply to the member state two years after the date of notification – unless a different date is agreed to before that date (by qualified majority and obtaining the consent of the European Parliament) or after that date (by unanimity).

During the period between notification and exit, the EU is required to negotiate and agree (by qualified majority and obtaining the consent of the European Parliament) with the member state the arrangements for its withdrawal and future relationship with the EU.

1   http://www.lisbon-treaty.org/wcm/the-lisbon-treaty/treaty-on -European-union-and-comments/title-6-final-provisions/137 -article-50.html (accessed 1 August 2013).

would not be to reject everything connected with Europe, but simply to regain the sovereignty to choose which aspects of the EU and European law should apply in the UK. The paper further assumes that the objective of the government upon exit is to promote a free and prosperous UK economy and that it would therefore wish to take steps to achieve this aim.

EXTERNAL NEGOTIATIONS

Trade and economic

One of the most critical factors in determining the UK's success following an exit from the EU will be its terms of trade, both with the EU and with the rest of the world (RoW). A sharp rise in tariffs to either party would not only be economically costly, but could deliver a symbolic blow far beyond its actual economic effect, leading to capital flight, loss of business confidence and a reduction in foreign direct investment. Any descent into protectionism by the UK would send similarly negative messages around the world, as well as directly harming UK competitiveness.

Trade with Europe

Even if current trends continue,[3] it is likely that until at least the end of this decade the EU will remain the UK's single most important trading partner. The highest economic priority should therefore be to ensure that zero tariffs are maintained on bilateral trade between the UK and the EU in all areas other than agriculture.[4] This would ideally be achieved by joining the European Free Trade Area (EFTA), similar to Norway, Iceland or Switzerland, but could also be achieved by joining European Union Customs Union (EUCU), similar to Turkey. Table 1 sets out the distinctions between these options in more detail.

While trade access is critical, full membership of the Single Market should not be sought. As Box 2 sets out in more detail, the Single Market is far more than just a customs union, or even a deep and comprehensive free-trade zone. Should the UK retain membership of the Single Market, almost all of the most onerous or controversial aspects of EU membership would continue to apply, including the free movement of people and the Working Time Directive. Accordingly, the UK should, unlike Norway, seek to remain outside the European Economic Area (EEA). The position sought should be somewhere between that of Turkey's and Switzerland's membership of EFTA but not of the European

---

3   As discussed in more depth below, the relative importance of the EU as a trading partner compared with the rest of the world has been decreasing year on year for at least the last decade.

4   The reasons for treating agriculture differently are explained below.

Table 1   Comparative positions of Norway, Switzerland and Turkey and proposed UK position after exit

Issue	Norway	Switzerland	Turkey	UK after exit (proposed)
Membership of EFTA	Yes	Yes	No	Yes
Membership of EEA	Yes	No	No	No
Membership of EUCU	No	No	Yes	No
Free movement of goods	Yes	Yes	Yes	Yes
Free movement of agricultural goods	No	No	No	No[a]
Free movement of services	Yes	Yes	No	Partial
Free movement of people	Yes	Yes	No	No
Free movement of capital	Yes	Yes	No	Yes
Contributes to EU budget	Yes	Yes	No	No[b]
Significant portions of EU law applied	Yes	Yes[c]	Partial	Partial[d]
Can negotiate own external trade agreements independently of EU	Yes[e]	Yes[e]	No	Yes[f]

[a] 'Yes' would be preferred but is almost certainly unachievable.
[b] An outcome in which the UK contributed minimally to a small number of specific programmes would be acceptable.
[c] Although not a member of the EEA, Switzerland has a series of over 100 bilateral agreements that largely duplicate the application of much of the *acquis communautaire* that would be applied if it were a member. See http://ec.europa. eu/trade/policy/countries-and-regions/countries/ switzerland/ (accessed 1 August 2013).
[d] 'No' would be preferred but is almost certainly unachievable if significant market access is also desired.
[e] Usually, though not required to do so, with other EFTA states.
[f] Though would usually do so with other EFTA states.

Economic Area (EEA) and without application of significant portions of EU law.

The UK will inevitably need to accept some EU regulation in order to gain the necessary trade access in both goods and services.[5] Financial services are a particularly critical sector: from

---

5   Trade in services, which makes up almost 40 per cent of total UK trade (ONS 2013), is of great importance to the UK. Full access for services is not practical – even now, the Single Market is not complete for services even for EU members – but access in the most important areas for UK exports would be important.

2019 onwards, providers outside the EEA will only be able to offer a more limited range of services, unless they establish a subsidiary within the EEA (House of Commons Library 2013). In addition to the impact on UK businesses, London currently benefits as the subsidiary location of choice for financial companies from countries outside the EEA such as the US and Switzerland. The UK should therefore seek to negotiate an exit agreement that will allow this access to be preserved, potentially accepting a certain degree of regulatory cooperation as the price for access.

The UK should also be prepared to accept regulation on standards for electronic machinery or for health and safety inspection requirements for food exports: many of these will be based on international standards and similar in type if not specifics to what exporters to other countries such as the US must abide by. There is no similar justification, however, once having left the EU, to accept regulation on purely internal matters such as working hours, hygiene requirements for domestic restaurants or mandatory quotas for women on boards.[6] A reasonable compromise between access and regulation might resemble the trade-off offered to members of the Eastern Partnership, who are expected to adopt approximately two-thirds of the *acquis communautaire*, though a successful negotiation could reduce the burden of regulation still further.

Trade with the rest of the world

For at least a decade the UK's exports have been shifting steadily towards the rest of the world rather than the EU27 (see Figure 1). Deepening those relationships will be of critical importance if the UK is to maintain its place as a major trading nation and economic power.

---

6   That is not to say that the UK might not choose to legislate on these matters domestically; however, this would be a matter for the UK Parliament.

Box 2   What is the Single Market?

The Single Market is far more than a customs union or a comprehensive free-trade agreement. The treaty that instigated the Single Market was not the Treaty of Rome, but the Single European Act of 1987, which was much more concerned with matters of economic integration.

At its most basic, the Single Market refers to the creation of an area in which there are no functional barriers to the free movement of goods, people, services and capital. Subsequent treaties have seen the addition of other areas, such as environmental, social and employment policy.

Regulatory harmonisation in these areas, and in others including health and safety regulation, environmental regulation, public procurement, infrastructure markets and standards, form a core part of the Single Market. It has been concluded that it is not possible to establish a clear division between member state and EU competence in the Single Market area: that any situation where there is a national regulation that could act to restrict movement of people, goods, services, or financial flows is potentially unlawful and subject to legal challenge (HM Government 2013).

A further significant aspect of the Single European Act was the introduction of Qualified Majority Voting – and the recent rejection of the UK's challenge of an EU ban on short selling was welcomed by the European Commission as having 'vindicated the use of a single market legal base, which requires approval of a weighted majority of member states, to empower the agencies'.[1]

Deepening the Single Market has been used to justify the regulation of how businesses conduct dispute resolution

---

1   http://www.ft.com/cms/s/0/68cbcb64-834c-11e3-aa6500144feab7de
.html (accessed 31 January 2014).

schemes, and the recognition of professional qualifications between member states. It has been behind issues such as metrication and the Working Time Directive. A recent Commission booklet[2] references subjects as diverse as patents, European bonds, access to capital and a common consolidated tax base.

While many individual aspects of the Single Market are beneficial, 'creating a level playing field for business' can ultimately be used to justify almost any intervention.

2   http://ec.europa.eu/internal_market/smact/docs/brochure -web_en.pdf (accessed 18 January 2014).

As a World Trade Organization (WTO) Member and signatory of the EU's free-trade agreements (FTAs) in its own right,[7] the UK will continue to be bound by these obligations and should expect other countries to reciprocate.[8] To do so would be in the interest of both parties: aside from the basic economic benefits of trade, continuing to honour their FTAs with the UK would require no additional negotiation and would maintain the status quo; to repudiate them would result in the raising of tariff barriers and increased costs for both exporters and importers in the partner countries as well as the UK. While it might not be a priority for all of these partners to negotiate an FTA with the UK if one did not exist already, maintaining an existing one would almost always be advantageous.

7   The UK, like all other EU member states, is a member in its own right of the WTO. Though currently its tariffs and services obligations are incorporated in the schedules for the EU, they would still stand as an obligation on the UK if the country exited the EU. Similarly, the UK signs and ratifies EU trade agreements in its own right, even though all negotiation is done by the Commission.

8   There may be technical complications, such as the UK being subject to EU dispute settlement procedures for these FTAs, but these would be an acceptable price to pay.

Table 2   Free trade agreements of Switzerland, Norway, New Zealand and the EU with non-EU G20 countries

	Argentina	Australia	Brazil	Canada	China	India	Indonesia	Japan	Mexico	Russia	Saudi Arabia	South Africa	South Korea	Turkey	US
Switzerland				✓	✓			✓	✓		✓[a]	✓[b]	✓	✓	
Norway					✓				✓		✓[c]	✓[d]	✓	✓	
New Zealand	✓				✓										
EU					✓				✓			✓	✓	✓[e]	

[a] As part of an agreement with the Gulf Cooperation Council.
[b] As part of an agreement with the Southern African Customs Union.
[c] As part of an agreement with the Gulf Cooperation Council.
[d] As part of an agreement with the Southern African Customs Union.
[e] As part of the EUCU.

Although in theory the situation could be resolved via legal means at the WTO Dispute Resolution Mechanism, it is not expected that this would be necessary. Nevertheless, this should not be taken for granted. An urgent dialogue with key trading partners should take place shortly after the referendum to establish the above as a common position and reaffirm the existence of FTAs. Simultaneously, the UK should attempt to establish FTAs with several other major trading nations.

As the experience of other small, developed trading nations such as Switzerland and New Zealand shows, the advantages of being unconstrained by the concerns of more protectionist EU member states and of a streamlined negotiating process should more than outweigh the disadvantages of reduced bargaining power (see Table 2). The UK could therefore enjoy a more favourable position than it enjoys within the EU, which to date has FTAs with not one of the BRIC countries.[9] For countries with

---

9   The EU has FTAs with many of the neighbourhood countries (including Turkey), South Africa, South Korea, Chile, Mexico and a number of Central American countries. Negotiations with India have yet to reach a conclusion, those with Mercosur

Figure 1   **Percentage of UK exports to the EU and ROW**

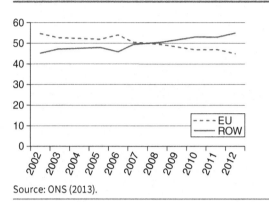

Source: ONS (2013).

which the EU is close to concluding negotiations,[10] the UK should seek to negotiate a side-agreement with the country concerned, whereby the UK was treated as part of the EU for the purposes of that specific trade agreement.

Priority of FTA negotiations

It is possible to rank the priority of forming an FTA with each of these countries using an analysis based on three factors: the volume of UK exports to that country, relative growth of UK exports over the last 10 years and average applied tariff imposed by that country. In addition to the 15 non-EU G20 members, the analysis also includes Hong Kong and Singapore as the only two non-G20 members to appear in the list of the UK's top-ten export destinations[11] (see Table 3). The full analysis is at Appendix A.

---

have stalled and those with the US and Japan are at an early stage. Negotiations for an FTA with China have not begun.

10 Which could potentially include the US or India, depending on the progress of current negotiations.

11 Though the data may not be fully representative due to many of the imports to these two countries being subsequently re-exported to other countries in the region.

Table 3 **The UK's top ten non-EU, non-EFTA export destinations (2012)**

Country	UK exports (£bn)
US	84.1
China	13.7
Australia	10.9
Japan	9.4
Canada	8.1
Russia	7.6
Saudi Arabia	7.5
Hong Kong	7.5
Singapore	7.2
India	6.9

The 17 countries can be categorised into three initial categories, of high, medium and low priority, as set out in Table 4.

The priority listing is necessarily limited and could be supplemented by more detailed econometric analysis that carried out dynamic modelling of the likely benefits of an FTA with these countries. In particular, the consideration of tariff data does not take into account the potential gains from trade in services, deeper integration and the elimination of non-tariff barriers, which would be likely to be of particular economic benefit in trade with other developed nations such as the US, Canada and Australia.[12] In consequence, the relative priority of these nations is likely to be underestimated and they should potentially be given a higher priority than suggested in the table.

Equally crucially, Table 4 does not take into account the political economy factors that will determine the relative likelihood of being able to successfully conclude FTA negotiations. Canada, Mexico, South Korea, Turkey and South Africa all have existing FTAs with the EU – it should be relatively simple to secure an agreement that the terms of these negotiations should continue to apply, as discussed above. Equally, some countries such as Argentina are unlikely to wish to negotiate an FTA with the UK in the near future due to other long-term issues of dispute that dominate the bilateral relationship. It should be noted that although an FTA with China or Russia would undoubtedly be challenging

---

12 For the UK, tariffs are roughly 0.5 per cent of the value of exports to the US, while NTBs are roughly 8.5 per cent of the value of exports to the US; over 90 per cent of the estimated gains from the Transatlantic Trade and Investment Partnership (TTIP) come from removal of NTBs (Centre for Economic Policy Research 2013).

due to these countries' economic power and outlook, the potential benefits make the attempt worthwhile.

Trade promotion

In addition to concluding FTAs, the government should continue to invest significant resources in trade promotion activities to assist individual firms export into new markets. This activity will be of most value in fast-growing, emerging markets that are not traditional export destinations – British businesses, particularly small- and medium-sized enterprises (SMEs), will typically need more assistance to do business in a country such as China or Vietnam than in the relatively familiar markets of the US or Germany.

The RBS research paper 'In search of export opportunities' considers a number of non-traditional markets against four axes – compatibility, growth, prosperity and ease of exporting – to conclude that in the 'attractive and large' category are countries such as China, Korea, Mexico, Turkey and Brazil. It also identifies a cluster of Latin American markets in its 'attractive but small' quadrant (RBS 2013). The number of countries included in the survey is limited, but, nevertheless, it does provide useful pointers.

It is clear that the ASEAN group of nations,[13] their northern neighbours such as Taiwan and South Korea, Latin America and the Gulf States are becoming increasingly important export markets.

Table 4 **Initial priority order for non-EU, non-EFTA FTA negotiations**

Priority	Countries
High	China
	Russia
Medium	Argentina
	Australia
	Brazil
	India
	South Korea
	US
Low	Canada
	Hong Kong
	Indonesia
	Japan
	Mexico
	Saudi Arabia
	Singapore
	South Africa
	Turkey

---

13 The UK already exports more to ASEAN than to either India or Japan: https://www.gov.uk/government/speeches/south-east-asia-forum (accessed 21 January 2014).

Assisting firms to do business in these markets will ensure that the UK secures a share of their growth. Efforts to shift attention from developed to emerging markets that are already underway in organisations such as the Foreign Office and UK Trade and Investment should be redoubled, with the necessary resources used to increase support for government-to-government deals, strengthen overseas business networks and help UK business win major opportunities with both the private and public sectors.

Other economic matters: agriculture, migration and science

Three further issues warrant explicit consideration: agriculture, migration and science.

Agriculture

It is unlikely that the UK would continue to enjoy duty-free access to the EU[14] in agriculture; nor would it be likely to be able to negotiate such access. In consequence, the UK's agricultural sector will need to rely much more significantly on the domestic market to survive.[15] To mitigate this, the government should maintain some degree of targeted subsidy for the sector and/or maintain external tariffs to Europe at the rate the EU chooses to impose them on the UK. Subsidies would result in a lower price of food for consumers and may therefore be politically, as well as economically, preferable.

---

14 Iceland, Norway, Switzerland and Turkey do not enjoy such access – agriculture is included in neither EFTA nor the EUCU. Though some of the countries in these agreements enjoy separate bilateral agreements in agriculture, all fall considerably short of duty-free, quota-free access.

15 Although the UK is a net food importer, it nevertheless exported over £12 billion of food and non-alcoholic drinks in 2012, approximately three quarters of which went to EU countries. See http://www.fdf.org.uk/exports/ukexports/topline _performance.aspx (accessed 6 September 2013).

Migration

The government should end the automatic right to free movement of EU citizens and treat future immigration from EU nations in the same way as immigration from outside the EU. The current situation constrains policy space in two significant ways.

Firstly, the fact that EU citizens can not only move to the UK but can then enjoy many of the benefits, from domestic-rated university fees to welfare payments, puts significant pressure on the public purse[16] and can reduce the ability of the government to devise policies that meet its objectives.[17] Notably, broader policies that a government might decide are desirable, such as free or subsidised university education or particular approaches on welfare, may be rendered unviable because free movement across the EU renders them liable to exploitation.

Secondly, given the domestic pressure to reduce net migration, free movement for EU citizens curtails the government's ability to devise migration policies that grant more access to individuals – from anywhere in the world – with the skills or potential to benefit the UK.

The UK should not, however, unduly antagonise the rest of Europe. Short-term, visa-less access for EU citizens should be maintained and reciprocal access negotiated. The government should also grant all EU citizens legally residing in the UK at the time of exit indefinite leave to remain and again should seek to obtain a reciprocal understanding from the rest of the EU.[18] Together, these changes would reclaim the necessary policy space

---

16 To take just one example, in 2011/12 nearly £104 million was paid in fee loans to EU students (House of Commons Library 2013).

17 For example: 'UK faces European Court over benefits for EU nationals': http://www.bbc.co.uk/news/uk-22712569 (accessed 3 September 2013).

18 Though whether they should have the right to continue to access public funds such as unemployment benefit or tuition fee support would be something the government should review, considering each type of benefit individually.

while maintaining the benefits of freedom of short-term travel throughout Europe.

Science

The UK benefits considerably through its participation in European science programmes such as the EU Framework Programme for Research and Innovation,[19] the European Space Agency (ESA) and the European Centre for Nuclear Research (CERN).

International science cooperation is both highly valuable and, for large-scale endeavours, can be more efficient, and the UK should aim to remain a full partner in all of these programmes. Membership of CERN would not be affected by the UK leaving the EU as it is not an EU organisation; similarly for the Framework Programme and ESA, non-EU membership should not be a bar.[20] While the UK would not automatically be a member, it should seek to secure its participation as part of the exit agreement or by applying separately, ideally between the date of the referendum result and exit from the EU.

Political

The UK is fortunate in that it is already a member in its own right of most international institutions: the G8, the G20, NATO, the OECD, the WTO, the United Nations Security Council, the Commonwealth and others. Leaving the EU should not alter this: the

---

19 In addition to the broader benefits of wider science collaboration, from a purely financial perspective the UK contributes around 11.5 per cent of the cost and wins 16 per cent of the funding available, a net gain. See https://theconversation.com/britain-should-stay-in-the-eu-for-science-18129 (accessed 24 January 2014).

20 Both Switzerland and Norway are members of ESA; Switzerland, Norway, Israel, Turkey, Croatia, the Former Yugoslav Republic of Macedonia, Serbia, Albania, Montenegro and Bosnia & Herzegovina are associate members of Framework Programme 7, contributing to the budget and with the same access to grants as EU countries. See http://cordis.europa.eu/fp7/who_en.html and www.esa.int/ (both accessed 17 January 2014).

UK is the world's sixth largest economy (World Bank 2013), has the fourth highest defence budget (SIPRI 2013) and is a significant contributor to the UN, IMF and World Bank. Nevertheless, it will be important for the UK to maintain or increase its engagement with these global institutions, to emphasise that the withdrawal from the EU is not a withdrawal from globalism. In particular, greater engagement with the OECD on global standards would pay economic dividends.

The UK should reinvigorate its engagement with those countries which share its desire for an open, transparent and rules-based international economic and political system. With less collaboration possible with the EU, the Foreign Office's resources should be increased to allow the UK to more effectively punch above its weight in the world, with a particular focus on the emerging powers.

In addition to the long-standing relationship with the US, strategic partnerships with countries similar to the UK in size should be cultivated, with significant commitment of senior ministerial or prime ministerial time. Australia and Canada would make natural partners on a wide range of issues from trade to global governance. A scoping exercise should also be conducted to identify other countries, particularly in South East Asia and Latin America, with whom Britain shares interests across a broad spectrum of issues.

Equally, the UK should not turn its back on Europe. Although Britain would be less able to collaborate with the Commission and other EU institutions, strong partnerships with individual member states could and should be maintained. Despite some differences on economic affairs, analysis of United Nations General Assembly (UNGA) voting patterns shows that in international affairs, the UK agrees with France more than with any other major nation (Ferdinand 2013). Recent close military and political cooperation on topics including Libya and Mali demonstrates the strength of this relationship.

Germany, the most economically powerful nation in the EU, is also an essential partner and should be treated no less favourably. The establishment of quarterly Heads of Government summits with each of these nations, with more frequent dialogue between cabinet ministers, would do much to cement these ties.

The UK should also seek to establish a formal 'EU out-group' of European countries which are outside the EU but have close trading arrangements with it, including all non-EU members of EFTA and the EUCU.[21] As befitting the diverse range of interests within this grouping, this would be a non-binding forum of independent nation states such as the OECD or the G8 rather than a supranational organisation like the EU. Such a mechanism would allow this grouping to speak with a strengthened voice in discussions with the EU and reduce the possibility of decisions being taken to the disadvantage of its members. In addition, it would provide an attractive outer circle of nations that could be joined by countries that wished close ties with the EU but did not wish or were not ready to pursue ever closer union, thereby helping to extend Europe and the UK's economic sphere of influence without compromising sovereignty.

European negotiating tactics

If handled correctly, the UK could be confident in achieving a positive result from the exit negotiations: whatever resentment is felt at the UK for leaving, an EU emerging from recession would not wish to stifle trade with one of its most significant trading partners. This, however, is not an inevitable outcome: while it is in no one's rational economic interests to erect trade barriers, the EU could afford a trade war far better than the UK could.

---

21 Iceland, Liechtenstein, Norway, Switzerland, Andorra, Monaco, San Marino and Turkey. Depending on the future development of the euro zone compared to the rest of the EU over the next two decades, such a group could ultimately evolve to include non-euro-zone members as well.

Some EU nations would see leaving as a betrayal of the European project and may wish to ensure that a sufficient example is made of the UK to deter others. It would therefore be necessary to take great care in the negotiations to both accommodate the domestic 'needs' of various nations as well as mollifying, at the most senior level, those who might harbour resentment.

As set out above, the exit agreement must be approved by a qualified majority of member states. However, some of the subsequent agreements that the UK might wish to include, such as membership of EFTA, would, for new members, need to be agreed unanimously by EFTA states. Whether qualified majority or unanimity is required for a current EU (and therefore EFTA) member seeking to 'downgrade' its membership from EU to EFTA status is a matter of legal debate (House of Commons Library 2013). It would, in any case, be preferable to have as strong as possible a majority among member states in order to overcome inevitable opposition in the European Commission and European Parliament, while continuing to maintain the legal position that a simple qualified majority is required.

The two highest priorities must be to secure EFTA (or equivalent) access to the European market and to regain full national sovereignty without threat of further political or financial integration. Most other factors are secondary; in particular, it would be worth agreeing to one-off or time-limited measures, such as continuing to pay the UK's EU budget contributions to the end of this budget period, or concessions for EU workers currently residing in the UK, in exchange for achieving the former objectives. Table 5 sets out a list of likely topics for negotiation and their priority.

Throughout the negotiations it must be remembered that the UK is in the weaker position: in the case of no agreement, the UK would face the full trade barriers that any external nation does. It is unlikely to be possible to simply 'park' economic matters, as joining EFTA – or the EUCU or the EEA – must be agreed upon by the EU and all its member states (see above). Brinksmanship by the UK could therefore be very costly. The UK should also take a conciliatory stance in all other EU negotiations ongoing at the time,[22] using these as an opportunity to win allies.

While a significant reallocation of UK officials currently working on EU affairs to exit negotiations is clearly necessary, the essential agreements to secure support would need to be done at the highest level, with significant investment of ministerial and prime ministerial time. For example, while the initial opening bid might be for full duty-free access in all goods, following a summit with the French president, the prime minister could agree to accept some agricultural tariffs in exchange for French support – which would likely bring with it that of other member states with large agricultural sectors such as Poland or Italy.

It would be critical to engage business organisations across Europe in making the case for an open trade settlement. Regardless of their views on whether the UK should leave, once the decision has been taken, bodies such as the Confederation of British Industry (CBI) and the British Chamber of Commerce (BCC) – and their sister organisations across Europe, such as Eurochambres or the Bundesverband der Deutschen Industrie – are unlikely to want trade stifled by the imposition of tariffs and non-tariff barriers (NTBs).[23]

Close cooperation between the government and domestic business organisations would support the establishment of a consistent and vocal call for open markets from European business, which would in turn encourage the governments of other EU member states to agree to maintain as open markets as is possible.[24]

---

22 Under the Lisbon Treaty a withdrawing state maintains full negotiation and voting rights until withdrawal itself in all dossiers other than the terms of its own withdrawal.

23 See, for example, http://www.cbi.org.uk/media-centre/press-releases/2013/09/ 8-out-of-10-firms-say-uk-must-stay-in-eu-cbi-yougov-survey/ (accessed 22 January 2014).

24 Again, this is unlikely to be effective in the agricultural sector, where domestic lobbies are overwhelmingly protectionist.

Table 5   Likely topics for negotiation in a UK exit agreement

Issue	Importance	Difficulty of achieving	Overall priority[a]
Regaining full national sovereignty[b]	High	Medium	High
Membership of EFTA[c]	High	Medium	High
Non-membership of EEA[d]	High	Medium/High	High
Ability to opt out of at least 1/3 of the *acquis*	High	Medium/High	High
Free movement of capital	Medium/High	Low	Medium/High
No free movement of people[e]	Medium/High	Medium	Medium/High
Significant access for services	High	Medium/High	Medium/High[f]
Reciprocal indefinite leave to remain for current residents	Low/Medium	Low/Medium	Medium[g]
No contribution to EU budget	Medium	Medium/High	Medium[h]
Access to EU Research Framework programme	Low/Medium	Low	Medium
Guarantees regarding the nature of Single Market regulation and its impact on EFTA members	Medium/High	High	Low/Medium[i]
Duty-free access for agricultural goods	Medium	High	Low/Medium[i]

[a] A higher importance and a lower difficulty of achieving both contribute to the overall priority.
[b] Including, in particular, autonomy from decisions of the European Court of Justice (ECJ).
[c] Which would remove all tariffs and quotas for non-agricultural goods while retaining the right for the UK to carry out its own trade agreements and to be not covered by significant sections of EU law.
[d] The EU may attempt to link membership of EFTA and the EEA.
[e] There would be no objection to granting visa free access though.
[f] There will be an inevitable trade-off between the amount of regulation accepted and the access for services. A balance should be struck, as long as it does not endanger higher objectives.
[g] A likely concession.
[h] It would be quite acceptable to agree a time-limited, tapering contribution, or contribution to specific programmes, or even a small permanent contribution (10–20 per cent of current contribution).
[i] Very unlikely to be achieved.

Germany would be one of the most likely nations to be pragmatic, but would not want to endanger the European project. The German Chancellor must be closely engaged throughout and, where possible, UK negotiating positions and compromise papers should be taken forward with German support. As the most economically influential nation in the EU, Germany would be an invaluable ally in forging a position that could be accepted by other nations. The Dutch and Nordic nations, traditional UK allies who may feel the most betrayed by a UK exit, have broadly similar economic and political positions to Germany and so would also be most likely to agree to proposals that have German support.

The eastern member states are most likely to be placated by a commitment to tapering off (as opposed to an immediate cessation) budget contributions, while many of the smaller member states may need to be 'bought off' with minor concessions in exchange for coming on board. The Commission and European Parliament are likely to be among the most hostile,[25] so securing a strong consensus with active support among member states would be essential in overcoming that inevitable resistance.[26]

Overall, a consensual, pragmatic approach to the negotiations would be essential, with the direct personal engagement of the prime minister and close cooperation with the most influential EU members in order to achieve a successful outcome.

INTERNAL PREPARATIONS

The fact that the UK is a member of neither the Euro nor the Schengen Zone will greatly simplify the needed preparations. The challenge of re-establishing an independent currency while preventing capital flight and maintaining open capital markets

---

25 Though the election of a greater number of Eurosceptic MEPs from across Europe in the 2014 European elections may alter this.

26 The Commission has no direct power over the negotiations, but considerable influence, both public and behind the scenes. The European Parliament may simply approve or veto – while of critical importance, ultimately it is unlikely to block an agreement that has the strong support of member states – particularly as many MEPs are at least somewhat responsive to their parent governments. Securing that firm consensus, one that, as in the recent budget negotiations can withstand and overcome parliamentary opposition, will be critical to success.

would be an unenviable task. Nevertheless, both legislatively and administratively, there will be a significant degree of preparation required.

Legislative

As soon as possible after the referendum, the government should introduce a 'Leaving the EU Bill' into Parliament. The government should prioritise parliamentary time for the Bill to reduce international and business uncertainty, while still allowing the necessary time for the extensive debate that such a Bill will require.[27]

The Bill should cover not only the necessary constitutional aspects of leaving the EU but should also make provision for the more pragmatic aspects of departure.[28] Given the likely need to introduce and pass the Bill before negotiations with the EU have concluded, the Bill should include a significant number of delegated powers, predominantly making use of the affirmative procedure,[29] to allow these issues to be determined after the EU-exit negotiations have concluded, subject to a final affirmatory vote of Parliament.[30]

---

27 As a highly significant Bill, it is likely that it will need to be debated by a Committee of the whole House.

28 For example, determining at what level tariffs will be set, issues concerning border controls and passports, transferral of administrative or regulatory functions currently carried out by the Commission and the continued rights of EU citizens currently in the UK.

29 Under the affirmative procedure, both Houses of Parliament must expressly approve the order.

30 This would function in a similar way to that in which the United States Congress may grant the President 'Fast Track Negotiating Authority' to conclude a trade agreement with a certain country, within certain parameters. The final agreement must be put back to Congress for approval, but can only be approved or denied, not amended. As described here, for example, http://www.bloomberg.com/news/2014-01-09/congressional-deal-reached-on-obama-trade-talks-authority.html (accessed 24 January 2014).

> **Box 3   Regulations and directives[1]**
>
> *Regulations* are legislative acts of the EU which have direct legal effect. As they are not replicated in domestic law, after exit from the EU the default position would be that these would no longer be binding.
>
> *Directives* are legislative acts of the EU which do not have direct legal effect, but rather set out an objective that must be achieved by each member state by means of devising its own laws to bring them into effect. As directives are implemented by Acts of the UK Parliament, these Acts would continue to have binding effect in the UK unless explicitly repealed, even though the directive itself would no longer be binding.
>
> ---
>
> 1   http://europa.eu/eu-law/decision-making/legal-acts/index_en.htm (accessed 17 January 2014).

One consideration is what should be done with the large number of existing EU regulations and directives (see Box 3). Such a high proportion of UK law has now originated from Brussels – the House of Commons Library (2010) considers 'it is possible to justify any measure between 15% and 50%' of total UK regulation as coming from EU – that to abolish it all could have significant undesirable and unforeseen consequences.[31] Yet to simply incorporate all EU law untouched would be missing a valuable opportunity for reform. In addition to simple repeals, operating outside the EU would allow regulation to be tailored to achieve the best results for the UK economy and society, rather than having to use regulations that are the result of compromise between 28 widely differing nations.

---

31 One would probably not wish, for example, to simply repeal Regulation (EC) No 178/2002 (which lays down the general principles and requirements of food law and procedures in matters of food safety) without first considering how to regulate food safety after it had been repealed.

The government should therefore bring forward a 'Great Repeal Bill', based in some respects on the principles of the Public Bodies Act (2011). The Great Repeal Bill would have three objectives:

* Incorporate certain selected existing EU regulations[32] temporarily into UK law from the date of exit.
* Within three years require the government to explicitly review all of these regulations, as well as any Acts of Parliament or UK secondary legislation that predominantly enacts an EU directive, to determine whether it is desirable that they continue in force.
* Provide that the government must, for each law listed in the Act, make a positive decision within the three-year period to retain the legislation by means of an Order brought forward under the super-affirmative procedure (see Box 4), or else the law will cease to apply.

Regulatory repeals

A non-exhaustive examination of EU regulation shows some clear potential candidates for repeal or reform.

Employment law

The Working Time Directive (2003/88EC) should be repealed. As well as increasing flexibility for both employers and employees, this would reduce bureaucracy in maintaining records of who

---

32 The expectation would be that only those regulations or parts of regulations which could be considered to apply in a purely domestic consequence, and where there seemed a risk of potential serious harm to the UK if they were to suddenly lapse, would be incorporated. Only regulations explicitly named would be incorporated. The majority of the *acquis communautaire* relevant to the four freedoms (free movement of goods, people, services and capital), as well as those pertinent to 'flanking policies' (i.e. transport, competition, social policy, consumer protection, environment, statistics and company law) would not be incorporated.

Box 4   Super-affirmative procedure[1]

Most secondary legislation is subject to either the negative procedure (in which the order comes into force unless Parliament votes against) or the affirmative procedure (in which both Houses of Parliament must expressly approve the order).

In rare cases, the super-affirmative procedure is used, which requires the minister to have regard to representations, House of Commons and House of Lords resolutions, and Committee recommendations that are made within 60 days of laying, in order to decide whether to proceed with the order and (if so) whether to do so as presented or in an amended form. The super-affirmative procedure was used for a number of procedures in the Public Bodies Act (2011), due to the extremely broad powers that the Act gave ministers concerning the abolition of a wide range of public bodies – a circumstance analogous to EU withdrawal, when a wide range of Acts and regulations would potentially be repealed.

---

1   http://www.parliament.uk/business/committees/committees
-archive/regulatory-reform-committee/regulatory-reform-orders/
(accessed 31 August 2013).

---

had opted out. Some of the provisions other than that governing the maximum working week – such as the need for rest periods or minimum paid annual leave – could be maintained, though a careful assessment should be made of whether any cause unreasonable burdens on business.

Sectoral provisions, including for fishing, offshore and transport workers should similarly be reviewed to ensure that these take into accounts the needs and pressures of these industries. Where not abolished these should be simplified: the current complexity (Box 5 gives an example) means that even where there is little impact on working patterns, the administration

---

Box 5   Excerpt from a summary of EU driving regulations for vehicles over 3.5 tonnes

---

The driver must not drive more than:

- 9 hours in a day – this can be extended to 10 hours twice a week.
- 56 hours in a week.
- 90 hours in any 2 consecutive weeks.
- All driving done under EU rules must be recorded on a tachograph.

The driver must take:

- At least 11 hours rest every day – this can be reduced to 9 hours rest 3 times in a week.
- An unbroken break of 45 hours every week – this can be reduced to 24 hours every other week.
- A weekly rest after 6 days of working – coach drivers on an international trip can take their weekly rest after 12 days; a break or breaks totalling at least 45 minutes after no more than 4.5 hours driving.

---

can cause a significant burden for large and small companies, as well as restricting the rights of employees to work as they would wish to.

Other areas of EU employment law should be examined carefully with a view to simplification and ensuring that they remain fit for purpose in the UK's labour market. The extensive provisions regarding consultation of workers' representatives in the Collective Redundancies Directive (98/59/EC), for example, appear outdated in the UK's increasingly non-unionised labour force.[33] Even where the protections are, in principle, considered

---

33 Around 6.5 million employees in the UK were trade union members in 2012, below the peak of over 13 million in 1979 (BIS 2013).

to be worth keeping, the administration and implementation should be simplified. The Agency Workers Directive (2008/104/EC) has increased the burden of hiring agency workers, reduced the flexibility that business has to hire people and should therefore be repealed or amended to give greater flexibility for individual employers and workers to reach their own arrangements.

Agriculture and environment

The recent EU practice of banning pesticides and fertilisers based on hazard[34] rather than risk should be changed: a reversion to a more scientific risk-based approach would prevent substances that are safe to use being banned and increase farming productivity.[35] Regaining regulatory control over genetically modified (GM) crops would allow the UK to better respond to future developments in the scientific evidence as to whether these can be safely grown.

The Waste Framework Directive (2008/98/EC) should be amended by removing the requirement for SMEs to register as waste carriers if they only transport a small amount of their own non-hazardous waste. This could benefit up to 460,000 small businesses in the UK (Business Taskforce 2013).

A wide range of environmental regulation, including the Waste Electrical and Electronic Equipment (WEEE) Directive (2002/96/EC), the Regulation on Registration, Evaluation, Authorisation and Restriction of Chemicals (REACH) (1907/2006/EC), the Directive on Packaging and Packaging Waste (94/62/EC) and the Water Framework Directive (2000/60/EC), among others, should be examined and, where possible, simplified.

---

34 Hazard is the severity of what could happen; risk is hazard multiplied by the likelihood of it happening.

35 See, for example, http://www.fwi.co.uk/articles/26/09/2013/141248/regulatory-threats-to-pesticides.htm (accessed 26 January 2014).

Many of these serve a useful purpose and should not be abolished without replacement; however, simplifying the administration, reporting and enforcement regimes could help to significantly reduce burdens on business.

Financial services

It would be important to ensure that domestic control was reasserted over areas of core economic interest such as the City of London. Regulations such as the Markets in Financial Instruments Directive (2004/39/EC), the Capital Requirements Directive IV (CRD 4)[36] and the Alternative Investment Fund Managers Directive (2011/61/EU), among many others should be scaled back to ensure that the UK does not face additional burdens beyond the standards set out in international agreements such as Basel III.

If specific legislation is needed beyond this to deal with any risks specific to the UK market, it should be implemented on a national level.

Energy and transport

Directive 2009/28/EC, establishing binding renewable energy targets for 2020, should be repealed. While it may be desirable to achieve these, establishing the matter in statute reduces the ability to appropriately respond to the evolving energy needs and environmental pressures in the UK. The energy performance of buildings (2010/31/EU) is also more appropriately the province of national legislation.

---

36 See Draft Implementing Technical Standards with regard to supervisory reporting of institutions according to Regulation (EU) No. 575/2013, which includes, among others, the cap on bankers' bonuses; http://ec.europa.eu/internal_market/bank/regcapital/legislation_in_force_en.htm#maincontentSec1 (accessed 17 January 2014).

There is much room for cooperation in transport, particularly in air transport and in the movements of goods. However, rules covering the rights of passengers (including 1177/2010/EU and 181/2011/EU), on driving time (2002/15/EC) and on the form in which driving licences must be issued (2006/126/EC), among others, could be reformed and simplified, particularly where the principles are established in other existing regulations.

Business and commercial law

The EU's permissive stance on jurisdictional 'forum shopping' should be reversed and, subject to limited exceptions, the fundamental English and common law tradition that the parties' choice of forum should be regarded as paramount reinstated.

Currently, within the EU it is no longer possible for an English court to prohibit by injunction the commencement of proceedings in an EU court even if it is in breach of a contractual choice of forum clause. This can allow litigants to significantly delay legal resolution by pre-emptively commencing proceedings in other EU nations with less efficient legal systems, which in turn adds to the legal costs of business and makes the UK a less attractive place to conduct major contractual deals.

If passed, the draft directive imposing mandatory quotas for women on boards (2012/0299 (COD)) should be reversed, as an unnecessary and potentially counterproductive measure that would be better served by non-legislative means combined with existing equalities legislation. Similarly, the decision of the ECJ (Test-Achats) which found that insurance and annuity providers could not take gender into account when determining the prices for their products should be reversed. Preventing providers of such risk-based products from utilising evidence-based risk factors weakens the operation of a true market in such products and could increase prices for all users.

The Prospectus Directive (2010/73/EU) places disproportionate burdens on the ability of small companies to make a public equity offer: for a £5m offering, the cost of producing a prospectus in the UK is estimated at between £350,000 and £600,000 (Business Taskforce 2013). This significantly inhibits and reduces the liquidity of the public (retail) investor market. Raising the exemption thresholds from €5m to €50m and from 150 to 2,000 shareholders[37] could make it easier for smaller companies to fund business growth.

Health and safety law

A wide range of EU health and safety regulations should be either repealed or reformed. The EU's summary page of legislation lists five general provisions and twenty-two specific provisions on product safety,[38] ranging from the Machinery Directive (2006/42/EC) to the Dangerous Products Resembling Foodstuffs Directive (87/357/EEC). Such a detailed and specific approach, attempting to legislate for each individual case, inevitably places a large burden on businesses, particularly SMEs, while being unable to deal with the full complexity of the market. A more principles-based legislative approach, in which all consumer products are required to meet a reasonable standard of safety with penalties for negligent or wilful transgression, would allow much of the more detailed and sector-specific European regulation to be repealed.

Where businesses are exporting to the EU they may reasonably be expected to demonstrate that they have met certain EU standards. However, while it is reasonable for a food exporter to have to comply with EU legislation on animal feed, there is no

---

37 Similar to the reforms recently carried out in the US.

38 http://europa.eu/legislation_summaries/consumers/consumer_safety/index_en.htm (accessed 17 January 2014).

good reason why businesses operating purely domestically, such as a restaurant or a community organisation, should have to comply with EU regulations.[39] This principle should be applied consistently when determining which regulations to repeal. In fact, even where a product can be exported, there is no reason that unnecessarily high EU standards or processes should be retained in EU legislation. Businesses that wish to export would be free to adopt the higher standards – including adopting these across their entire production process if this is simpler and cheaper – while SMEs that are producing only for a local or regional market would not be required to. To avoid any possibility of double regulation for exporters, compliance with the relevant EU legislation would be considered sufficient (but not necessary) to count as following the principles of any domestic principles-based legislation.

The Health and Safety at Work Framework Directive (89/391/EEC) requires all businesses to keep written records of risk assessments carried out in their workplace, regardless of risk. Either repealing or modifying it to exempt small businesses working in low-risk sectors would benefit at least 220,000 UK small businesses (Business Taskforce 2013).

Consumer law

A similar principle should be adopted as for health and safety regulation in order to free domestic business or non-exporters from regulations such as Textile Products Regulation (1007/2011/EU) and the Labelling of Foodstuffs Regulation (1169/2011/EU). National legislation would need to replace some of the requirements contained in these, particularly the latter, but the adoption of a principles-based approach would simplify the burden across

---

39 Such as the Food and Feed Safety Regulation (178/2002/EC).

different sectors. Cooperation could helpfully be maintained on cross-border issues such as roaming charges and cross-border bank payments.

The Unfair Commercial Practices Directive (2005/29/EC) could potentially be largely retained without alteration as it largely adheres to the principles-based approach advocated above. However, some of the supporting pieces of regulation, notably the recently adopted regulations on Consumer Alternative Dispute Resolution (2013/11/EU) and Online Dispute Resolution (524/2013/EU) which require, among other things, all businesses to offer recourse to an independent entity that offers out-of-court dispute resolution for all disputes, both domestically and across borders, should be abolished as unnecessarily burdensome.

Conclusion

The above analysis is simply a brief glance at the over 3,000 pieces of EU legislation[40] that currently exist to give an indication of some of the areas where reforms and repeals could be implemented. It is not intended to be comprehensive, nor does it necessarily identify the most egregious pieces of legislation. A thorough review would be essential in order to achieve the most positive outcome.

Which exact pieces of regulation are repealed will be a political decision for the government of the day. As long as some meaningful repeals take place, this will succeed in lightening the burden on businesses, the public sector and third sector, as well as for individuals.[41]

---

40 http://europa.eu/legislation_summaries/index_en.htm contains over 3,000 summaries of EU legislation (accessed 17 January 2014).

41 The British Chamber of Commerce estimates that the annual burden of EU regulation introduced since 1998 is £7.5 billion (British Chamber of Commerce 2010).

Administrative

Some sectors and regions of the UK currently benefit from various EU schemes including the Common Agricultural Policy, the European Framework Programme for Research and Innovation and the European Regional Development Fund (see Figure 2). A sharp reduction in this funding would cause an undesirable shock to those sectors and regions. The government should therefore, after exiting, increase proportionately the programme budgets of the relevant departments to ensure that these sectors and regions receive no immediate drop in funding. Following this, the budgets of these departments can be tensioned as normal, but from the new baseline.

Figure 2   **How does the UK spend the money it receives from the EU?**

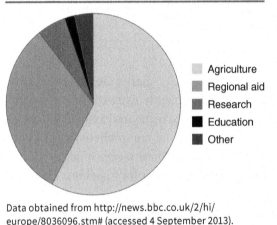

- Agriculture
- Regional aid
- Research
- Education
- Other

Data obtained from http://news.bbc.co.uk/2/hi/europe/8036096.stm# (accessed 4 September 2013).

Given that the UK is a net contributor to the EU, after reallocating funds in this way, the government will have a surplus of approximately £10 billion.[42] While much of this could be used simply to reduce the budget deficit,[43] some will need to be spent to increase the UK's administrative capacity in areas that had previously been solely or primarily the competence of the EU.

42 Net of receipts under the CAP, EU regional funding, and the budget rebate, the government contributed £10 billion to the EU in 2012 (House of Commons Library 2013).

43 The Office of Budget Responsibility forecasts that the UK will have a budget deficit until at least 2018 (OBR 2013).

Trade, in particular, is an area that would need to be significantly enhanced: the UK has essentially no external negotiating capacity as trade negotiations are conducted entirely by the European Commission. It will be particularly important to bolster this capacity if the UK is to be able to rapidly conclude FTAs with major emerging powers (see above).

In other areas, from anti-trust enforcement to fisheries policy, UK agencies will need to have their capabilities increased – though, equally, the UK should have no shame in simply pronouncing that in certain matters it will follow the EU's lead.[44] Where possible, the UK should seek to build expertise by inviting back UK nationals from the relevant branches of the Commission, paying enhanced salaries where appropriate for skills and experience that cannot currently be obtained within the UK civil service.[45]

Judicial

The complexities of exiting from several decades of EU law and EU jurisprudence will not be easily overcome. Some laws and regulations may simply be abolished, but in cases where the same or similar laws remain in place, important questions must be answered, including whether UK courts remain bound by precedent set by the European Court of Justice (ECJ) prior to the UK's exit, or whether UK judges should pay heed to future interpretations of EU judges when similar laws may remain in place in both jurisdictions – such as competition law. Unless positively

---

44 There is no reason, for example, why the UK should feel the need to conduct its own inquiries into the safety of global airlines, when it could instead simply co-opt the list of banned airlines maintained by the Commission.

45 It is an open question as to whether UK nationals currently working in the Commission would be permitted to continue working there following a UK exit. If UK nationals were forced to leave, then the UK might benefit from the sudden pool of recruitable talent; on the other hand, if nationals were allowed to remain in place it could be a means of continuing to have some influence.

addressed as a whole by Parliament, the judiciary will be forced to fill the vacuum via ad hoc decisions on individual cases, which is undesirable.

The government should therefore establish a cross-party commission, similar to the Parliamentary Commission on Banking Standards,[46] populated by some of the most influential and informed members of both the House of Commons and House of Lords, to set out the outline of a Bill that would clarify the situation and reassert unambiguously the supremacy of UK law and British courts.[47] Although technically distinct from the question of leaving the EU, it would also be helpful for the commission to consider the matter of the European Court of Human Rights (ECtHR) and the interaction of UK courts with this institution. The commission should be tasked with reporting shortly after the date of the UK's exit from the EU, with a view to the government introducing a Bill in the following parliamentary session.

Inward investment

A significant risk of a UK exit is a drop in the quantity of Foreign Direct Investment (FDI) coming to the UK, which currently makes a significant contribution to jobs and economic activity.[48] While it is not possible to say definitively the extent to which membership of the EU is a factor in inward investment decisions, it is undoubtedly a factor. Furthermore, in the two years between the referendum and exit, the uncertainty created by the unknown trading relationship with the EU could cause businesses (both external and internal investors) to delay investment decisions until this is resolved.

---

46 http://www.parliament.uk/bankingstandards (accessed 23 December 2013).

47 The review and any Bill would need to explicitly take into account the very different legal systems prevailing in England and Wales, Scotland and Northern Ireland.

48 In 2012/13, 1559 inward investment projects created or secured over 170,000 jobs (UKTI 2013).

As soon as the exit agreement with the EU is agreed, the UK government should therefore conduct a strong and sustained outwards campaign to communicate the reality of the terms of the exit. This will be essential if the UK is to maintain its position as the number one destination for FDI in Europe.[49] The UK's attractiveness for FDI, and its value as a gateway to Europe, will remain strong,[50] and the UK's fundamentals – including liberalised energy and employment markets, ease of raising capital and ease of starting a business – will be as strong as ever.[51] The repeal of selected European regulation to create an even more business-friendly environment, together with the new security of the City of London from external interference,[52] will only strengthen this; however, by itself, such a campaign may not be sufficient to maintain the current high levels of FDI.

In a 2013 survey of over 2,000 multinationals, 72 per cent of companies interviewed in North America and 66 per cent of those in Asia thought reduced integration with the EU would make the UK more attractive as a destination, against 38 per cent of those interviewed in Western Europe (Ernst and Young 2013). Accordingly, the government should, after exit, quickly put in place policies to capitalise on this viewpoint and actively encourage inward investment. These should include some or all of the following:

---

49 In 2012 the UK was the largest recipient of net FDI in Europe, receiving net inflows of over $62 billion (UNCTAD 2013).

50 Any investor for whom use of the euro is essential will already be going elsewhere.

51 The UK is currently considered the 10th most competitive country in the world (World Economic Forum 2013). Switzerland, a non-EU European country is ranked 1st.

52 Professor Philip Booth of the Institute of Economic Affairs has said that 'The danger is another financial centre could take London's place' and that 'The pernicious aspect of EU legislation is, it seems, to be intended to promote protectionism and driven by ignorance and suspicion of those who make money from finance': http://www.thisismoney.co.uk/money/markets/article-2313153/CITY-FOCUS-Londons-status-global-financial-centre-challenged-abroad.html (accessed 5 September 2013).

- A stepwise lowering of the rate of corporation tax to 15 per cent over 5 years.[53]
- Extend the period in which losses can be offset against profits for new investors.
- Establish sector strategies for key industries, developed in collaboration with business, with a particular focus on maintaining and developing the supply chain, to encourage investment in those areas which will most benefit industries in which the UK has existing strengths.
- Create special economic zones in poorer regions of the UK, offering incentives to investors such as a 12-month employer's National Insurance holiday or tax breaks. Such zones have had a demonstrated impact in countries as varied as the Dominican Republic, Taiwan and Vietnam,[54] provided they have been well aligned with the country's overall economic policy framework and comparative advantage.
- Increase the R&D tax credit for new investors by 25 per cent over the standard rates for two years after investing, to encourage investment and job creation in high value, knowledge intensive industries.
- Implement flanking policies that support an attractive investment climate, in particular investing in adequate new transport infrastructure, investing in sufficient generating capacity to provide affordable power and ensuring the planning regime is fit for purpose.
- Where appropriate, negotiate international agreements on foreign direct investment, something which the UK has not been able to do since the Lisbon Treaty came into force in 2009.

---

53 It is assumed that the rate of corporation tax at the time of exit is 20 per cent.

54 http://www.voxeu.org/article/special-economic-zones-what-have-we -learned (accessed 26 January 2014).

Even with such measures, there will probably be an inevitable dip, due to the uncertainty surrounding the exit; however, following this there is no reason why the volume of FDI should not fully recover and even increase further.

OUTCOMES

It is difficult to determine with certainty the overall costs and benefits of exit: reputable organisations have found the cost/benefit of EU membership to be anywhere from −5 per cent to +6 per cent of GDP (House of Commons Library 2013). Though being in the EU offers benefits, being outside may offer just as many, ranging from a reduction in regulation and a reduced cost to the Exchequer to a greater ability to conclude trade agreements with the major emerging economies. In particular it is very difficult to accurately estimate dynamic effects, such as the long-term impact of trade creation or of reduced regulation increasing the competitiveness of business.

The existing shift in the UK's trade pattern from the EU to the rest of the world will accelerate, as weaker ties to the EU are combined with new trade agreements with emerging powers. Such a shift will stand the UK in good stead as the balance of world growth shifts eastwards and south.[55]

Much will depend on the success of the exit negotiations with the EU and with other potential trading partners, the steps taken domestically to ease the burden of regulation and the reaction of world markets and international business. Below are set out 'best-case', 'most probable' and 'worst-case' scenarios for the UK's situation three to five years after the referendum (one to three years after exit), though it should be emphasised that nothing can be predicted with certainty.

---

55 EU GDP growth has consistently lagged world GDP growth by approximately 2–3 per cent per annum for the last decade. See http://www.indexmundi.com/g/g.aspx?c=xx&v=66 (accessed 4 September 2013).

Scenarios

Best-case scenario

The UK negotiates a generous exit agreement with the EU, securing EFTA access, including some concessions for agriculture, and access for significant service exports in exchange for accepting half or less of the *acquis*. Undiminished trade access and a halving of the regulatory burden imposed by the EU on business cause exports to boom, fuelled additionally by a range of new agreements with major and mid-sized external trading partners including China, Brazil, Russia, Australia and India. Existing EU trading partners maintain their FTAs with the UK, some with minor amendments. The reduction in the regulatory burden and a competitive tax environment more than compensate for EU exit, causing foreign investment to increase slightly. Total impact on GDP is estimated at +1.1 per cent.

Most probable scenario

The UK negotiates a satisfactory exit agreement with the EU, securing EFTA access and access for significant service exports in exchange for accepting approximately two thirds of the *acquis*. Regulatory reforms free up business to operate more competitively and contributions to the EU are gradually phased out over a period of five years, though the UK continues to contribute to a small number of common programmes.

Existing EU trading partners maintain their FTAs with the UK, some with minor amendments, and the UK also secures new agreements with several mid-level trading partners such as Australia and Brazil, though negotiations go more slowly with China, the US and Russia.

After some initial market wobbles, the stable trading relationship with the EU reassures international business and the positive steps taken to promote investment ensure within two years inward investment levels have regained their pre-exit levels. Total impact on GDP is +0.1 per cent.

Worst-case scenario

The UK fails to negotiate an acceptable exit agreement with the EU and withdraws with no agreement in place. All access to the Single Market is lost and the UK exporters must pay the full 'most favoured nation' (MFN)[56] tariffs paid by other developed nations. No other trade agreements are signed and some major nations with FTAs with the EU, including Canada and South Korea, refuse to honour theirs with the UK. Without the ability to export tariff free to the UK, inward investment plummets, while international money markets react badly, causing the UK's borrowing costs to spike. Both exports and imports fall. Contributions to the EU cease. With no exit agreement in place, the UK is free to cut burdensome regulation and does so significantly, but this is not enough to mitigate the impact of the other outcomes. Total impact on GDP is –2.6 per cent.

In total, the impact of each of the three scenarios is given in Table 6. Appendix B provides the full working for how the GDP changes in each scenario have been calculated.

Although the most likely scenario shows a small positive gain, it should be emphasised that this should not be taken to mean that a UK exit would automatically be a good thing. The +0.1 per cent gain is well within the margin of error for such estimations and, in any case, the high degree of variance between the best- and worst-case scenarios means that a positive outcome could not be guaranteed. Ultimately, the decision of whether or not the UK should remain within the EU is a political rather than an economic one.

---

56 The tariffs imposed by the EU on nations with which it does not have a preferential trading agreement such as an FTA.

Table 6   Impact on GDP of the best-case, most likely and worst-case scenarios

	Best case	Most likely	Worst case
EU trade (£bn)	−7.7	−9.3	−19.2
External trade (£bn)	5.6	2.1	−1.8
Budget contribution (£bn)	10.0	6.0	10.0
Regulatory (£bn)	3.8	2.5	3.8
FDI (£bn)	4.5	0.0	−15.6
Debt interest (£bn)	0.0	0.0	−17.2
Total gain or loss (£bn)	16.1	1.3	−40.0
Total gain or loss (%GDP)	1.1%	0.1%	−2.6%

Avoiding and mitigating the worst-case scenario

The most likely scenario may be economically acceptable; however, what if the worst case occurs? The aspect that is least within the UK's control is whether or not the rest of the EU will permit continued preferential trading arrangements – whether through membership of EFTA, the EUCU or some other bilateral special agreement. As discussed earlier, securing this should be the primary objective of the negotiations; however, it must be acknowledged that there is a non-zero risk that such an agreement will not have been put in place by the time the UK leaves the EU. In such a scenario there are two possibilities: firstly that the negotiations are proceeding well, but that slightly more time is needed to finalise the exact details; or, secondly, that there has been a repeat of De Gaulle's 'Non' and one or more powerful member states has explicitly blocked the UK's entry into a preferential trading arrangement.

In the first instance, the UK should take all possible steps to conclude the agreement as rapidly as possible. In the interim, the UK's current MFN tariffs should be applied to EU goods (and the EU will undoubtedly do the same to UK exports): this will have an immediate impact on business, thereby creating strong pressure from the private sector on both sides of the Channel to conclude negotiations swiftly. Individual bilateral discussions, at cabinet or prime ministerial level and in person rather than by phone where possible, should be held with any recalcitrant member states who are blocking a deal to see what concessions they desire: this should be given a high priority and the strong presumption should be that any minor concessions for special industrial interests should be accepted.

As soon as these are completed – within three months or six at the most – the Presidency should be asked to put forward a compromise proposal incorporating these amendments, which could then be approved by the Council and European Parliament.

In the second case, the UK must prepare for an indefinite period with no special access to the EU market. While not absolutely disastrous – the total trade weighted applied average tariff of the EU is only 2.7 per cent[57] – it would undoubtedly have a significant impact on large segments of UK industry and on GDP as a whole. Furthermore, it would materially decrease the UK's attractiveness as a destination for overseas investment as such investors would no longer have duty-free access to the EU.[58]

To some extent, mitigation involves taking the same steps that would be taken in the event of any UK exit and redoubling them. Securing trade access with external partners, encouraging inward investment and slashing business regulation to promote competitiveness all become even more critical to make up for the loss of access to EU markets.

In addition, the UK should put in place temporary subsidies for those sectors that will be most impacted by the imposition on EU

---

57 31.2 per cent of agricultural products and 26.1 per cent of non-agricultural products (by value) have an applied MFN tariff of 0; the total applied tariff (WTO 2013).

58 In November 2013 the CEO of Nissan said that 'Nissan will reconsider its investment in the UK' if Britain leaves the EU – http://www.bbc.co.uk/news/business-24859486 (accessed 26 January 2014).

tariffs.[59] These subsidies should be strictly time-limited, tapering and aimed at helping those industries to improve their competitiveness and export to new markets outside the EU. This would prevent them fostering inefficiency and rent-seeking behaviour.

With respect to the EU, the UK should impose the same MFN tariffs that other developed exporters face. Notwithstanding the theoretical positive economic case for unilaterally removing tariff barriers,[60] it is important that shutting the UK out of EU markets is not a cost-free decision for continental business, in order to build the environment for a future deal once the political climate has altered.[61] The UK should not, however, seek to unduly antagonise the EU via restrictive measures such as safeguards and, as far as possible, should seek to decouple other matters – such as regulatory cooperation or rights for EU citizens currently domiciled in the UK and vice versa – from the failed negotiations on trade. Needless to say, without trade access the UK should accept none of the *acquis* and should make no contribution to the EU budget.

CONCLUSION

It is abundantly clear that the UK can have a positive economic future either inside or outside the EU. Canada, a smaller economy than the UK,[62] prospers alongside its much larger neighbour, the United States; New Zealand has forged a successful nation despite its decision not to join with Australia in the late 19th

---

59 Such as alcoholic beverages or the automotive sector, both of which are key UK export sectors and where EU tariffs are relatively high.

60 In its pure form, the theory of comparative advantage indicates unilateral tariff removal is beneficial – a practical manifestation of which, in this case, is that tariffs on imports of intermediate goods from the EU would increase costs for manufacturers.

61 In addition, imposing anything other than MFN tariffs would violate the UK's WTO obligations.

62 $1.797 trillion for Canada compared to $2.443 trillion for the UK (CIA 2014).

century.[63] The UK is a modern, developed economy of almost 65 million people, the sixth largest economy in the world[64] with strong international alliances. While close economic and diplomatic relations with other European countries are both inevitable and to be greatly welcomed, this does not imply that membership of the EU is the only way these can be achieved.

What is equally apparent is that a UK exit from the EU would result in different costs and opportunities than a path of ever closer union. Many of these costs are an inevitable consequence – even if joining EFTA provided at least some degree of reduced access to the Single Market – meaning that appropriate policies and wise negotiation must be carried out if the UK is to reap the benefits. Whatever the arrangement, there is likely to be a trade-off between the level of access to the Single Market, and freedom from EU product regulations, social and employment legislation, and budgetary contributions (House of Commons Library 2013).

Throughout, the theme of this paper has been that the UK's policies after exit should embrace openness: openness to global trade, openness to worldwide diplomatic partners, openness to international business and investment. Domestically, reforms should take advantage of the freedom from European regulation while preserving common standards and cooperation where this is in the UK's best interests.

Nothing can be guaranteed – but that is true both inside and outside the EU. It is not in the UK's gift as to whether its major trading partners will agree to new FTAs, though rational self-interest on their part implies that, if the negotiations are conducted sensibly, at least some will succeed.

---

63 The counterfactuals, clearly, cannot be properly evaluated. One cannot say what Canada or New Zealand's GDP per capita would be if they were part, respectively, of the United States or Australia; however, one can definitively say that all four of the nations discussed are successful, developed countries which provide a good standard of life for their citizens.

64 http://data.worldbank.org/data-catalog/GDP-ranking-table (accessed on 4 September 2013).

Equally, we cannot be sure that remaining part of the EU would prevent the EU from bringing forward legislation that would directly disadvantage UK industry – EU membership has not prevented the recent implementation of a succession of financial services legislation, against the UK's wishes.[65]

It is probably inevitable that the couple of years immediately surrounding the exit would feature some degree of market uncertainty and fluctuating economic performance, while the terms of the UK's exit are decided. The initial actions to ensure a strong and prosperous UK must be begun during that time. The challenge would be to ensure that the UK can gain sufficient advantages – new trade partners, sufficient access to EU markets, minimal further contributions to the EU budget, an attractive investment climate and a reduced regulatory burden – to compensate for the loss of access to Europe and the loss of its voice in Brussels.

If the policies in this paper are adopted, five to ten years after the date of exit it is likely that the pattern and structure of the UK's trade and economy would have shifted to reflect a greater global outlook, with greater bilateral trade with the emerging powers of the world and with the US. The EU would continue to be a major trade partner, perhaps the single most important, but probably with a share closer to 30 per cent of the UK's trade than its current 48 per cent.[66] In international politics the UK would

---

65 In the last two years the UK has challenged at least four new EU financial regulations as having the potential to significantly impinge on the success of the City of London: short selling rules, the imposition of a financial transaction tax, the cap on bankers' bonuses and the European Central Bank's policy on providing liquidity to clearing houses. The first challenge was thrown out in January 2014; at the time of writing the others remain to be ruled on. See, for example, http://www.ft.com/intl/cms/s/0/68cbcb64-834c-11e3aa6500144feab7de.html#axzz2rpSgbVR1 (accessed 30 January 2014).

66 The EU's market share of total UK trade fell steadily between 2002 and 2012 by 11 percentage points, from 59 per cent to 48 per cent. Extrapolating this trend with no change for another 10 years would see it at 37 per cent. Exiting the EU could be expected to increase the trend, perhaps by 50–100 per cent, which would leave the EU's market share at approximately 30 per cent.

continue to punch above its weight, working with a wide range of allies both European, Commonwealth and others, though – like all other developed nations – it would be affected by the global shift of power from north and west to east and south.

Domestically, one would expect to see a nation of less and simpler regulation and a lower budget deficit, but that remained a beacon for foreign investment, albeit with rather more investors from North America and Asia and rather fewer from Western Europe. Its character – that of a global nation open to the world – would be unchanged. Overall, the UK would probably be neither significantly richer nor poorer: there is no recorded correlation between EU membership and GDP growth. The fundamental assets of the country, its population, global connections, infrastructure and knowledge base mean that the economic outlook should remain strong.

Ultimately, whether or not the UK exits from the EU is a political, not an economic decision. A wide range of factors, in particular the ideological question over where sovereignty should reside, will be at the heart of any future referendum. This paper does not, therefore, address the question of whether the UK should leave, or advocate for or against such a course of action. What it does do is demonstrate that, in the event of such an exit, there exists a scenario for an open, prosperous and globally engaged UK that is eminently achievable.

Appendix A: Analysis of trade policy options

This appendix sets out the analytical data and calculations behind the recommendations on trade negotiations.

Considering the analysis carried out above regarding the non-EU, non-EFTA, members of the G20, let us consider with which of these countries might lie the strongest interest for the UK in forming FTAs. To these 15 countries, we will also add Hong Kong and Singapore, as these are the only two of the UK's top 10 non-EU, non-EFTA export destinations that are not in the G20 (see Table 3).

To determine where the greatest advantage to the UK might lie in forming FTAs, we will consider each country against three criteria:

- Total volume of UK exports to that country in 2012.
- Growth of UK exports to that country relative to the overall trend of UK exports.
- Average applied tariff imposed by the country.

Each country will receive 0, 1 or 2 points in each of these three categories.

Export volume

Exports to each of the 17 countries and, for comparative purposes, to the EU and to the whole world are set out in Table 7.

A country is allocated 2 points for an export volume of over £10 billion, 1 point for £5–10 billion and 0 points for <£5 billion. It should be noted that exports to the US are, at £84 billion, over six times larger than those to the second largest export destination, China. Therefore, exceptionally, the US shall receive 3 points in this category.[67]

Growth

In addition to the absolute volume of exports, it is important to consider the trend of how the UK's exports to that country are growing. Any exit from the EU will be several years in the future; furthermore, in signing FTAs the UK should consider the future as well as the present.

---

67 This is justified: the size of the market makes it a significant outlier and it has been estimated that an FTA with the USA, as part of the TTIP, would be worth up to £10 billion annually to the UK (CEPR 2013), compared to the £0.5 billion it gained from an FTA with South Korea.

Table 7   UK exports (goods and services) 2002–12 (£bn)

	2002	2003	2004	2005	2006	2007	2008	2009	2010	2011	2012
Argentina	0.20	0.21	0.31	0.26	0.33	0.38	0.48	0.43	0.62	0.72	0.62
Australia	3.93	4.34	4.76	5.46	5.54	6.08	7.48	7.55	8.77	10.26	10.87
Brazil	1.18	1.15	1.10	1.23	1.45	1.55	2.34	2.54	3.13	3.74	4.17
Canada	4.59	4.81	5.08	5.09	6.06	6.12	6.43	6.79	7.73	8.82	8.09
China	2.19	2.80	3.64	4.25	4.91	5.33	7.60	7.60	10.30	12.43	13.67
Hong Kong	3.45	3.67	3.74	4.48	4.26	4.40	5.89	5.55	6.18	7.38	7.47
India	2.36	2.98	3.22	4.00	4.47	4.71	5.92	4.65	6.18	8.30	6.89
Indonesia	0.50	0.62	0.59	0.57	0.63	0.58	0.68	0.74	0.85	1.05	1.08
Japan	7.39	7.67	8.12	8.49	8.79	8.64	9.11	8.41	8.88	9.89	9.43
Mexico	0.95	0.95	0.97	0.95	1.17	1.16	1.31	1.24	1.47	1.56	1.68
Russia	1.56	2.14	2.37	3.04	3.85	4.96	6.51	4.31	5.26	7.20	7.58
Saudi Arabia	3.33	4.19	4.17	3.96	4.39	4.30	4.34	4.78	5.67	5.38	7.50
Singapore	2.59	3.25	3.89	4.90	5.55	5.97	6.47	6.98	7.23	7.79	7.16
South Africa	2.58	2.85	2.95	3.26	3.65	3.75	4.32	3.87	4.77	5.45	4.96
South Korea	1.97	1.94	2.39	2.45	2.67	2.84	3.69	3.13	3.51	4.05	6.37
Turkey	1.71	2.08	2.31	2.72	3.08	3.13	3.36	3.32	4.42	5.19	4.79
USA	50.50	53.10	54.49	56.76	63.64	68.72	73.32	70.38	77.55	81.46	84.08
World	280.00	293.08	305.82	339.84	387.59	380.52	429.76	402.17	447.27	492.88	492.81
EU	153.42	154.93	159.57	176.08	209.93	191.13	213.01	193.60	210.74	231.97	222.13

Data from ONS Pink Book 2013.

Table 8   UK trade export growth (goods and services), 2002–12

Country	UK exports 2002 (£bn)	UK exports 2012 (£bn)	Growth	Normalised growth
Argentina	0.20	0.62	204%	73%
Australia	3.93	10.87	177%	57%
Brazil	1.18	4.17	252%	100%
Canada	4.59	8.09	76%	0%
China	2.19	13.67	524%	255%
India	2.36	6.89	192%	66%
Indonesia	0.50	1.08	119%	24%
Japan	7.39	9.43	28%	–27%
Mexico	0.95	1.68	77%	1%
Russia	1.56	7.58	387%	177%
Saudi Arabia	3.33	7.50	125%	28%
South Africa	2.58	4.96	92%	9%
South Korea	1.97	6.37	224%	84%
Turkey	1.71	4.79	180%	59%
USA	50.50	84.08	67%	–5%
Singapore	2.59	7.16	177%	57%
Hong Kong	3.45	7.47	116%	23%
World	280.00	492.81	76%	0%
EU	153.42	222.13	45%	–18%

Exports to all 17 of the countries have increased over the 2002–12 period; however, for more appropriate comparison, we will consider how exports to each of the countries have grown when set against the overall growth of UK exports (a 76 per cent increase over the period). Table 8 sets out the data.[68]

---

68 Normalised growth figures scale the actual growth rate for the country concerned by the overall growth of UK exports (76 per cent), so a growth of 76 per cent would show as 0 per cent.

A country is allocated 0 points for an export growth of <50 per cent above trend, 1 point for 50–99 per cent above trend and 2 points for export growth of 100 per cent or greater above trend.

Average applied tariff

For each of the 17 countries, we consider the average applied tariff, using data from the WTO. Considering the average applied tariff gives an indication of how much UK exporters stand to gain from an FTA: if applied tariffs are very low, they will benefit less than if tariffs are high.

A country is allocated 0 points for an average applied tariff of <5 per cent, 1 point for an average applied tariff of 5–9.9 per cent and 2 points for an average applied tariff of 10 per cent or above.

Summary

After allocating all points, each country is allocated into a category of low, medium or high priority for formation of an FTA, as set out in Table 9. This gives rise to the priority order set out in the earlier section on trade with the rest of the world, where the findings are discussed further.

Appendix B: Analysis of outcomes

As discussed in the section on outcomes, it is hard to determine with certainty the overall costs and benefits of exit. In particular, it is very difficult, even with detailed economic modelling, to accurately estimate dynamic effects, such as the long-term impact of trade creation or of reduced regulation increasing the competitiveness of business. Nevertheless it is possible to clearly identify certain areas in which one can be confident that a UK exit will have an impact and to estimate how large that impact will be.

Table 9   FTA priority conclusions

Country	Volume	Growth	Tariffs	Total	Category
Argentina	0	1	2	3	Medium
Australia	2	1	0	3	Medium
Brazil	0	2	2	4	Medium
Canada	1	0	0	1	Low
China	2	2	1	5	High
Hong Kong	1	0	0	1	Low
India	1	1	2	4	Medium
Indonesia	0	0	1	1	Low
Japan	1	0	0	1	Low
Mexico	0	0	1	1	Low
Russia	1	2	2	5	High
Saudi Arabia	1	0	1	2	Low
Singapore	1	1	0	2	Low
South Africa	0	0	1	1	Low
South Korea	1	1	2	4	Medium
Turkey	0	1	1	2	Low
US	3	0	0	3	Medium

Throughout this appendix, UK GDP in 2012 is taken as $2,440 billion or £1,510 billion and the dollar/pound exchange rate as 1.615.[69] In all cases, the analysis considers the steady-state scenario, after any immediate transitional period is over.

Trade with Europe

In the time available it has not been possible to construct a detailed economic model of how much trade with Europe would be affected by a UK exit. Instead, the impact is modelled by considering the predicted impact of another trade agreement, the

---

69 GDP figure from http://www.tradingeconomics.com/united-kingdom/gdp (accessed 5 January 2014); exchange rate as at 5 January 2014, http://www.oanda.com/currency/converter/

Table 10   Cost of UK exit as calculated by comparison with the TTIP

	Benefit of TTIP (%GDP)	Benefit of TTIP (£bn, 2012)	Cost of UK exit (£bn)
Best case / 'Basic Modest'	0.14%	2.12	7.67
Most likely / 'Modified Modest'	0.17%	2.57	9.32
Worst case / 'Modified Ambitious'	0.35%	5.29	19.18

Transatlantic Trade and Investment Partnership (TTIP) on the UK and relating this to the EU.

The TTIP can be considered a reasonable model for the UK trading relationship with the EU for the following reasons:

* The US and the EU are the UK's two largest trading partners – both will have a significant impact on the UK's overall trading patterns.
* The US and EU are both highly developed economies with low external tariffs.
* The TTIP is proposed as a deep integration FTA, tackling issues such as NTBs, procurement and regulatory issues, similar to the UK's relationship with the EU.

The paper prepared by the Centre for Economic Policy Research (2013) for the UK government to model the impact of the TTIP employs a Computable General Equilibrium (CGE) model to analyse a number of scenarios for the final shape of the TTIP and estimates the benefit to the UK of each.

Taken in reverse, these scenarios are likely to be comparable to the costs to the UK of leaving the EU. One can model the 'basic modest' scenario as the best-case scenario for a UK exit (relatively little disruption), the 'modified modest' scenario as the most likely scenario[70] and the 'modified ambitious' as being broadly

---

70 As set out above, the most likely and best-case scenarios are relatively similar in terms of the trade access achieved; the difference being that in the most likely scenario the UK is forced to pay a higher price, in terms of regulatory cooperation and ongoing contributions than in the best case.

equivalent to the worst-case scenario (full reversion to MFN tariffs; significant erection of NTBs).

In order to complete the analysis, it is necessary to scale up the impact to account for the greater importance of the EU compared to the US as a UK trading partner.[71] The final costs are set out in Table 10.[72]

Trade with the rest of the world

In a similar manner, it is not possible to accurately model all possible combinations of external trade agreements in the different scenarios – particularly as the benefit to the UK would vary dramatically depending on not only the country but the nature of the FTA. Instead, an estimation has been done in a similar manner to the above, by equating possible future trade agreements to the benefit to the UK from the EU-Canada FTA (£1.3 billion annually[73]) for FTAs with developed countries and to the benefit to the UK from the EU-Korea FTA (£500 million annually[74]) for FTAs with emerging countries, appropriately scaled for their importance as a trading partner to the UK. Although the figures will not be exact, one can be confident that they will be of the right order of magnitude.

In the worst-case scenario, it is assumed that not only does the UK not manage to form any new FTAs, but that some of the

---

71 The scaling factor = (UK balance of trade with EU) / (UK balance of trade with US) = 488,667 / 134,709 = 3.628 (data from ONS Pink Book 2013).

72 It should also be noted that the pound costs given in the research paper are for a 2027 baseline. In order to ensure consistency with the figures used throughout the rest of this appendix, the fractional GDP figures are instead used and then converted into pounds at a 2012 baseline.

73 https://www.gov.uk/government/news/government-welcomes-historic-eu -canada-free-trade-agreement

74 http://blog.ukti.gov.uk/2010/10/25/why-the-eu-korea-fta-is-a-breakthrough-for -british-business/

Table 11   **UK benefit or loss from selected FTAs**

FTA	Equate to	Scaling factor	Annual value to UK (£bn)
South Korea	N/A	N/A	0.5
Canada	N/A	N/A	1.3
Australia	Canada	1.03	1.33
India	South Korea	1.52	0.76
Brazil	South Korea	0.70	0.35
China	South Korea	4.60	2.30
Russia	South Korea	1.67	0.83

countries which have signed FTAs with the EU – in the calculations assumed to be Canada and South Korea[75] – refuse to honour these commitments. In the most likely scenario, it is assumed that existing partners honour their commitments and that the UK also forms new FTAs with a small number of mid-sized[76] trading partners – for calculation purposes, taken to be Australia, India and Brazil.[77] In the best-case scenario, it is assumed furthermore that the UK succeeds in concluding FTAs with two major trading partners, China and Russia, in addition to the FTAs formed in the most likely scenario.

Table 11 sets out the amount that could be gained or lost from each FTA.

Using these values, the worst-case scenario results in an annual loss of £1.8 billion, the most likely scenario in an annual gain of £2.1 billion and the best-case scenario an annual gain of £5.6 billion.

75 The choice of these countries is not intended to imply they are more likely than other partners to renege on their commitments; they are simply a representative pair.

76 In terms of their importance to the UK as trading partners.

77 Again, a representative sample.

EU budget contribution

The net contribution of the UK to the EU was, in 2012, £10 billion annually (House of Commons Library 2013). Under the best-case scenario, the UK would cease all payments, a saving of £10 billion. The same is equally true under the worst-case scenario, as there would be no agreement with the EU. Under the most likely scenario, it is assumed that some residual payments would continue to be required, as a price for certain market access or for participation in certain programmes. This is modelled at 40 per cent of the current payments, or £4 billion annually, resulting in a saving of £6 billion annually.[78]

Regulatory

The burden of EU regulation is estimated at £7.5 billion annually (British Chamber of Commerce 2010). Not all of this regulation will be bad; therefore, one would not expect it to all be eliminated. Nevertheless, a significant economic gain from leaving the EU would be to lighten the burden of regulation.

Under the most likely scenario, it is assumed that the UK is required to accept approximately two thirds of the *acquis*,[79] which is modelled as two thirds of the cost of regulation, a saving of £2.5 billion. Under the best-case scenario, it is assumed that the UK only needs to accept the regulation it wishes to, which is estimated at around half – a saving of £3.75 billion. Under the worst-case scenario, as there would be no agreement with the EU, the UK again only needs to apply the regulation it wishes to, so the saving is again calculated as £3.75 billion.

---

78 The contribution of Switzerland, an EFTA but not EEA member, is 60 per cent less per capita than that of the UK (House of Commons Library 2013). As this paper proposes a considerably looser partnership with the EU than Switzerland's, a 60 per cent reduction may be considered a reasonable lower bound to the reduction.

79 In line with members of the Eastern Partnership.

Foreign direct investment

At £790 billion in 2012, the UK has the second largest stock of inward investment in the world, behind the United States, with average net inflows of £44.5 billion over the three preceding years (IMF 2013). It is very difficult to determine how much of this is as a result of the UK's membership of the EU – many other factors such as a favourable business climate, language and flexible labour law will play a strong part. Equally, it is hard to estimate how much difference measures that could only be put in place as a result of leaving the EU, such as reduced regulation, could compensate for any negative impacts of a UK exit. The evidence is equivocal: 72 per cent of companies interviewed in North America and 66 per cent of those in Asia thought reduced integration with the EU would make the UK more attractive as a destination, against 38 per cent of those interviewed in western Europe.[80]

In the most probable scenario, this will therefore be modelled as no change in FDI: essentially assuming that, after the transitional periods, the positives will balance the negatives. In the best-case scenario, it is assumed that the UK becomes even more attractive, with FDI increasing by 10 per cent. In the worst-case scenario, a recent survey by the CBI found that 35 per cent of firms would decrease their own business investment in the case of a UK exit (CBI 2013). It is notable that the benefit of EU membership cited most frequently by these firms (76 per cent of them) was the ability to buy and sell products without taxes and tariffs on trade flows in EU markets and only in the worst-case scenario would this no longer be the case. It is therefore assumed that, in the worst-case scenario, FDI decreases by 35 per cent.

---

80 Ernst and Young (2013). Across the whole world, 47 per cent considered it would make the UK more attractive and 47 per cent that it would make it less attractive.

Table 12   Impact on GDP of the best-case, most likely and worst-case
scenarios

	Best case	Most likely	Worst case
EU trade (£bn)	−7.7	−9.3	−19.2
External trade (£bn)	5.6	2.1	−1.8
Budget contribution (£bn)	10.0	6.0	10.0
Regulatory (£bn)	3.8	2.5	3.8
FDI (£bn)	4.5	0.0	−15.6
Debt interest (£bn)	0.0	0.0	−17.2
Total gain or loss (£bn)	16.1	1.3	−40.0
Total gain or loss (%GDP)	1.1%	0.1%	−2.6%

The impact of FDI on GDP is complex and can vary dramatically depending on the nature and sector of the investment.
However, given the openness of the UK to FDI and the mobility of
global capital, it is possible to simplistically model FDI as simply
part of the investment component of the GDP equation.[81] Drops
or increases in FDI are therefore modelled simply as drops or increases in GDP, giving a best-case impact of £4.5 billion, a most
probable impact of 0 and a worst-case impact of −£15.6 billion.

Debt interest

Under a worst-case scenario, in which a UK exit went badly leading to a crisis of confidence in the UK's ability to service its debts,
the cost of interest on the national debt would rise. This is modelled as a 1.5 per cent rise in interest rates. Taking national debt
as 75.9 per cent of GDP in 2018/19 (OBR 2013), a 1.5 per cent rate
increase would cost £17.2 billion at 2012 prices.

Under the best-case and most likely scenarios it is assumed
that such a crisis is avoided and so the cost of this effect is zero.

---

81   GDP = private consumption + gross investment + government spending + (exports
– imports).

Conclusion

Summing the above effects, the total impact in each of the three scenarios is set out in Table 12.

References

BIS (Department of Business, Innovation and Skills) (2013) Trade Union Membership 2012: Statistical Bulletin.

British Chambers of Commerce (2010) *Burden Barometer.* London: BCC.

Business Taskforce (2013) *Cut EU Red Tape: Report from the Business Taskforce.* London: BIS.

CEPR (Centre for Economic Policy Research) (2013) *Estimating the Economic Impact on the UK of a Transatlantic Trade and Investment Partnership (TTIP) Agreement between the European Union and the United States.* London: CEPR.

CIA (Central Intelligence Agency) (2014) CIA World Factbook. https://www.cia.gov/library/publications/the-world-factbook/

Ernst and Young (2013) *UK 2013: No Room for Complacency. Ernst and Young's Attractiveness Survey.* London: Ernst and Young.

Ferdinand, P. (2013) The positions of Russia and China at the UN Security Council in the light of recent crises. Security and Defence Sub-Committee of the EU Parliament.

HM Government (2013) *Review of the Balance of Competences between the United Kingdom and the European Union: Single Market.* London: HM Government (Cabinet Office).

House of Commons Library (2010) How much legislation comes from Europe? Research Paper 10/62.

House of Commons Library (2013) Leaving the EU. Research Paper 13/43.

IMF (International Monetary Fund) (2013) Coordinated Direct Investment Survey. http://www.imf.org/external/np/sta/cdis/

OBR (Office of Budget Responsibility) (2013) *Economic and Fiscal Outlook.* December 2013. London: OBR.

ONS (Office of National Statistics) (2013) *United Kingdom Balance of Payments – The Pink Book, 2013*. London: ONS.

RBS (Royal Bank of Scotland) (2013) In search of export opportunities. RBS Group.

SIPRI (Stockholm International Peace Research Institute) (2013) Military Expenditure Database. http://www.sipri.org/research/arma ments/milex/milex_database

UKTI (UK Trade and Investment) (2013) *Inward Investment Report, 2012/2013*. London: UKTI.

UNCTAD (United Nations Conference on Trade and Development) (2013) *World Investment Report 2013*. Geneva: UNCTAD.

World Bank (2013) GDP ranking. http://data.worldbank.org/data-cata log/GDP-ranking-table

World Economic Forum (2013) *Global Competitiveness Report 2013–14*. Geneva: World Economic Forum.

WTO (World Trade Organization) (2013) International trade and market access data. http://www.wto.org/english/res_e/statis_e/statis_e .htm

2 BRITAIN'S POST-EU FUTURE AND THE DEVELOPMENT OF EFTA PLUS

Robert Oulds

Introduction

Just as everyone wants equitable alimony arrangements after a divorce, an equitable free trade agreement is the ultimate goal of any discussions on Britain leaving the European Union. However, for the EU, trade with its neighbours is never free. Given the high volume and complexity of British trade, a fair deal could take as long as a decade to come into force. Negotiations are not just a matter of what the UK wants. The EU remains the single biggest jurisdiction to which the UK exports its goods and services and there are the views of the EU's other trading partners to take into account.

Under present EU thinking, which is unlikely to change given the EU's vested interests, there is little scope for an agreement that allows the UK to opt out of EU standards, many of which actually originate from above the EU and would be applied regardless of our EU membership. In the short term, it would make far more sense to reform existing architecture than attempt the immediate establishment of a new trade agreement or the creation of a new organisation that cannot be unilaterally delivered.

There is no need to reinvent the wheel, or invent new political movements, for off-the-shelf alternatives to EU membership already exist.

Retaining UK membership of the European Economic Area (EEA) will not only take advantage of existing institutions but also of other current trends and movements. The European Commission acknowledges the role that the EEA can play as an alternative to EU membership. Similarly, EFTA recognises its future role in a new European settlement.

It has been stated that before the UK leaves the EU a referendum will be held. If this plebiscite is to be won by the supporters of Brexit, then a number of commitments will need to be made and a clear exit plan developed. These political considerations, as well as economic necessity, will limit the UK's negotiating team's freedom of manoeuvre and leave only one tenable option that will have to be adopted immediately after Brexit. This option would a commitment for the UK to rejoin the European Free Trade Association (EFTA) and retain membership of the EEA. This, however, is not the end of the story. It would be the first step of an evolving relationship between Britain, the rest of the EU and other independent European states and overseas nations.

The EU and 'free' trade

From the perspective of the European Commission, free trade agreements are not just to encourage trade in goods but also intended to help export its regulations. A condition of reduced or tariff-free trade and the faster transit through customs is for non-EU states to apply common technical and health and safety standards. There are also the requirements to comply with environmental rules, ostensibly to ensure that competition is not being distorted by state intervention, that public procurement is open to all and that intellectual property rights are protected. The conditionality of EU trade deals even goes as far as to stipulate that the EU's human rights standards are adhered to.[1] This policy has found acceptance at the World Trade Organization (WTO). The EU's immediate neighbours are increasingly being

---

1   http://ec.europa.eu/trade/policy/countries-and-regions/agreements/#_europe

required to enter framework agreements with the EU. This is not just the case for members of the EEA but applies to Switzerland and beyond. Although Articles 3 and 8 of the Treaty on European Union legally require the EU to negotiate free and fair trade with non-EU countries, the EU considers it 'fair' only when other countries are competing in a similar regulatory environment.

There is therefore a price to be paid for accessing the EU's internal market from outside the EU. This may especially be the case for the UK if it leaves the EU.

Certainly, there is the possibility of recriminations. Herman van Rompuy, as the then President of the European Council, while recognising that the EU has a withdrawal clause and that exit is thus legally permissible, stated on 28 February 2013 in London that its secession will

> be legally and politically a most complicated and unpractical affair. Just think of a divorce after forty years of marriage ... But let us not dramatise. It is natural that all member countries can, and do, have particular requests and needs – and these are always taken into consideration.

In the same speech, he added, 'Leaving is an act of free will, and perfectly legitimate, but it doesn't come for free.'

The European Commission's advice to the European Council may well include recommendations that do not favour the UK. In addition, the European Council or Parliament could reject a reasonable withdrawal agreement or future free trade deal. This would not be the first time that politics have pre-empted economic common sense. The most significant costs on exporters will be customs levies; the threat of anti-dumping action; passing through a designated port of entry; clearing customs checks that will involve checking paperwork relating to rules of origin and making sure standards are applied; and loss of influence in the EU committees that draft legislation forcing the UK to accept

EU rules and apply their conditionality, which will require that a proportion of the *acquis communautaire* is adhered to. There is also the issue of UK-based companies being denied access to the EU's services market and public procurement.

So if there is a price to pay for leaving, the question becomes, 'How can the practicalities be smoothed and any potential damage be mitigated while exploiting the potential benefits of a future outside the EU?'

Aims and objectives: the desired outcomes of negotiations with the EU

Retaining full access to the Single Market in services needs to be a key objective. Membership of the EEA allows businesses to sell their services across the EU and in Iceland, Liechtenstein and Norway. This is of particular benefit to the UK with its strong services industry. The government believes that when the EU completes the Single Market in services – opening up all member states to competition – economic output could be boosted by as much as 7 per cent.[2]

The services industry is an especially important part of the UK's economic links with the EU. In 2011 the UK's trade in goods with the EU was in deficit by around £43 billion; however, trade in services was in surplus by £16 billion.[3] (See Figure 3.)

Swiss-based companies do not have the right to sell their services to the EU unless they establish a subsidiary inside the European Economic Area. This is not an insurmountable problem but should be avoided. Multinational companies by definition can and do establish themselves in different jurisdictions.

---

2   Department for Business Innovation and Skills, BIS Economics Paper No. 11, The economic consequences for the UK and the EU of completing the Single Market, February 2011, page vi: http://www.bis.gov.uk/assets/BISCore/economics-and-statistics/docs/E/11-517-economic-consequences-of-completing-single-market.pdf

3   http://www.theyworkforyou.com/lords/?id=2012-11-14a.1507.0

Figure 3   UK trade balance with EU in goods and in services

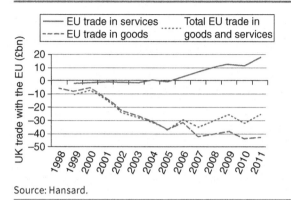

Source: Hansard.

However, small- and medium-sized enterprises will find creating subsidiaries burdensome in the EU's internal market, restricting opportunities.

Membership of the EEA also gives firms in all member states access to a market in public procurement alone – worth €2,150 billion per year – that in 2008 was around 16 per cent of the EU's entire GDP.[4]

Mutual recognition among EU and EEA member states is also important. Regulation EC 764/2008 of 9 July 2008 demands that all goods that are legally sold in one country can be sold in another. If the UK were outside this framework, British exporters would have to submit to more tests and red tape.

If there were no free trade deal, UK trade to the EU would be subject to tariffs in some areas. If tariffs were not levied on UK exports to the EU we would become, in WTO terms, a 'Most Favoured Nation'. This would mean that every other WTO state could lobby to have the EU's tariffs against their products struck down. The EU is not yet politically ready to completely liberalise

---

4   http://www.efta.int/eea/policy-areas/goods/competition-aid-procurement-ipr/
     procurement

trade with the rest of the world, even though it has a proliferation of free and preferential trade agreements. Many of these agreements contain conditions that apply EU standards. One key tariff is on the importation of cars (up to a maximum of 9.8 per cent[5]) though it is worth noting that the EU is actually a declining market for car sales. Yet not all EU states have a trade surplus with Britain. Vested interests in some EU members may not want to open up their markets to imports from third countries that enter tariff free via the UK.

Customs levies are not the only means by which the EU manipulates the price of goods in the internal market. There may also be anti-dumping measures on selected imports. Dumping is an aggressive pricing policy where exports to a foreign market are sold not only cheaper than the price in the domestic market but sometimes actually below the cost of production.[6] However, while anti-dumping action can be taken against the non-EU EEA states, the Commission does not usually target their produce.

In fact, anti-dumping measures are a double-edged sword. While they protect home-grown businesses they also risk a trade war with the state whose business suffers from their imposition. They raise the costs of imports making prices for consumers higher. Even the fear of them being imposed can encourage an importer to increase its prices. Professor Patrick Minford, of Cardiff Business School, estimates that this aggressive anti-dumping strategy amounts to a 'Common Manufacturing Policy', which is an attack on competition and allows for the creation of home-grown EU cartels which further increase prices. The cost to the UK may be according to Professor Minford as much as £30 billion per year (Minford et al. 2005). Outside the EU the UK still has the option of imposing anti-dumping measures if it so wishes

---

5   http://tariffdata.wto.org/TariffList.aspx

6   Council Regulation (EC) No 384/96 of 22 December 1995 on protection against dumped imports from countries not members of the European Community.

but it will give Britain a choice and create a consumer market with more competitive pricing without the use of anti-dumping measures.

When exporting goods to another territory the importing nation can stipulate a designated port of entry. At present, Britain and the European Union is one trade zone and the UK has free access. If Britain leaves the EU, the EU would have the hypothetical ability in the short term to prescribe a port of entry, and terms that are inconvenient for British exporters. However, this would be a breach of international trade law. Articles XI:1, XIII:1, V:2, V:6 and I:1 of the 1994 General Agreement on Tariffs and Trade are now administered by the WTO. Under these rules one country cannot be treated less favourably than any other in the export and transit of goods. However, cases of discrimination do still happen. What is more, there is still the need to reach an agreement and to initiate protection under the WTO regime and the UK will need to have its trade schedules formally approved by the WTO. Without these being approved it can be argued that the UK will not have its membership of the WTO reactivated.[7,8]

Will any ill feeling created by the UK leaving the EU damage British trade beyond the costs of the tariff to imports from outside the EU? This is unlikely. Even without the WTO, commerce will continue and economic self-interest would prevent the EU from overtly discriminating against British exporters. However, the limited potential for surreptitious prejudicial treatment of UK goods, such as delaying their clearing through customs, remains possible in the short term. All non-EU companies that export to the EU must complete paperwork and clear customs.

---

7 Trade and Investment Law Clinic Papers, The Future of the United Kingdom in Europe: Exit Scenarios and their Implications on Trade Relations, Katrin Fernekeß, Solveiga Palevičienė and Manu Thadikkaran, Geneva, 7 January 2014.

8 http://www.wto.org/english/tratop_e/schedules_e/goods_schedules_e.htm

Even if a free trade agreement is in place, customs will check that goods comply with rules of origin. EU membership frees exporters from having to prove the origin of the goods they are selling. The requirement to clear customs and complete documentation to validate the origin of goods and confirm that they are free from tariffs, applies even to Turkey. This country is a member of the EU's customs union and therefore has tariff-free access for industrial products but it is not bureaucracy-free access.[9] EU standards must also be applied by Turkey.

Negotiations under the Article 50: the EU's prescribed method of withdrawal

This analysis is predicated upon two assumptions: the UK has given notice to withdraw from the EU (the EEA requires separate notice to leave); and that this has been invoked after a referendum. This latter point can have important consequences.

Article 50 of the EU's constitution makes it clear that a member state can leave the European Union. The article goes on to decree that, 'In the light of the guidelines provided by the European Council, the Union shall negotiate and conclude an agreement with that State, setting out the arrangements for its withdrawal, taking account of the framework for its future relationship with the Union.'

This compels the EU, initially with the European Commission and later with the European Council acting upon recommendations from the Commission, to begin negotiations to reach agreement on the subsequent association between the EU and the exiting state. What form would this agreement take?

The Treaty on European Union (TEU) suggests an answer: Article 3 5 states that among other things: 'In its relations with the wider world, the Union shall uphold and promote ... free and fair

---

9   http://eur-lex.europa.eu/LexUriServ/LexUriServ.do?uri=OJ:L:2006:265:0018:0038
    :en:PDF

trade...'. Furthermore, Article 8 1 states: 'The Union shall develop a special relationship with neighbouring countries, aiming to establish an area of prosperity and good neighbourliness, founded on the values of the Union and characterised by close and peaceful relations based on cooperation.'

The withdrawal agreement should establish a relationship between Britain and the EU that is primarily based on trade and related issues including the UK's continued participation in continent-wide student programmes and other pan-European projects.

However, there are many complex issues that will need to be resolved. Even agreeing a new trade relationship alone will give the UK responsibilities as well as rights. The UK may wish to pass legislation allowing for the recognition of other countries' goods and standards and agree to the elimination of tariffs on trade between Britain and the EU. This agreement will therefore need to be ratified by both Houses of Parliament and be given the Royal Assent.

The UK's withdrawal will not be dependent solely on ratifying the agreement in the UK Parliament. If it is not agreed or is rejected by Parliament, then withdrawal, without resolving any outstanding issues, will still take place.

Difficulties with Article 50 will most probably appear before any vote in the British Parliament. Indeed, negotiations with the EU may not be that straightforward. Article 50 2 states that: 'agreement shall be negotiated in accordance with Article 218(3)[10] of the Treaty on the Functioning of the European Union. It shall be concluded on behalf of the Union by the Council, acting by a qualified majority, after obtaining the consent of the European Parliament.'

Therefore, the agreement under which a nation withdraws has to be approved by both the European Parliament and the Council and can be voted down. Negotiations with the members of the Council, representing the nation states, will in all likelihood be

---

10 Article 218 (Treaty on the Functioning of the European Union).

cordial, as it will be in every country's interest to keep good relations. Here the culture on consensus building in the EU can work in Britain's favour.

The need to gain the consent of the European Parliament is where problems with Article 50 are likely to emerge. While some MEPs may be glad to see Britain leave the EU, its membership is largely wedded to the principle of 'ever-closer union' and does not take kindly to setbacks to the process of European integration. Any agreement will need the approval of the European Parliament, indeed an absolute majority of MEPs (376 of 751) will have to vote for the terms of withdrawal. This is a high hurdle to pass. It will be best to remove them from the equation as much as is possible. This can be done by using existing alternatives to EU membership rather than negotiating a new bespoke agreement.

Nevertheless, if an agreement is not reached, then two years after the notice to withdraw is given, the departing state will be out of the European Union. It can also be out as soon as an agreement is in place.

Failure to reach a withdrawal agreement would, however, not be a good outcome for British exporters. Section 3 affirms that 'The Treaties shall cease to apply to the State in question from the date of entry into force of the withdrawal agreement or, failing that, two years after the notification referred to in paragraph 2, unless the European Council, in agreement with the Member State concerned, unanimously decides to extend this period.' And the fourth section reads: 'For the purposes of paragraphs 2 and 3, the member of the European Council or of the Council representing the withdrawing Member State shall not participate in the discussions of the European Council or Council or in decisions concerning it.'

This all limits the UK's negotiating hand, especially as the UK will not have a vote on the potential agreement. Such exclusion will put the remaining EU members in the driving seat and give them a greater ability to set the terms of the divorce. However, paragraph 4 of Article 50 does not prevent British MEPs from taking part in the withdrawal discussions and voting in the European Parliament on it. This fourth section finishes by establishing that 'A qualified majority shall be defined in accordance with Article 238 (3) (b) of the Treaty on the Functioning of the European Union.'

The exclusion of the withdrawing state from the Council discussions appears iniquitous. It allows opportunities for the EU to avoid reasonable conditions which would otherwise set a precedent for others wishing to leave. However, the terms would have to be agreed by the UK and therefore cannot be excessively onerous otherwise there will be no agreement.

As the EU lurches from one crisis to another, and given the complexities of the issues, it could take much longer than two years to work out the terms of a trade agreement. What is more, there is every possibility that the European Parliament will not agree to a withdrawal agreement that would allow the UK a preferential trade agreement. Even members of the European Commission have criticised the European Parliament for its insistence on adding to the EU's legislative morass. A member of the Commission Legal Service (Bellis 2003) has protested: 'The European Parliament, under the co-decision [ordinary] procedure, is allowed to propose uninformed, irrational, impractical amendments, safe in the knowledge that they have no responsibility for implementation.'

The two-year deadline for withdrawal can be extended – with the unanimous agreement of the European Council. Given the level of mistrust in British politics relating to EU issues, it would be politically untenable for a UK government to delay. There is also no mechanism for cancelling an Article 50 notification, only for extending the period of negotiations. However, the European Council will have to unanimously agree to the extension, the possibility therefore arises that an extension will be vetoed forcing the withdrawal to take place with no agreement.

If no agreement is in place and the UK is ejected, it would obviously require a backstop. Continued membership of the European Economic Area (EEA) offers the best guarantee of continued access to the Single Market. Rejoining the European Free Trade Association (EFTA) would also help secure a firm basis for continued negotiations with the EU.

EU law post-Brexit

Section 18 of the European Union Act 2011 reaffirms the view that EU law is only directly applicable through the European Communities Act. However, as a result of the European Union (Amendment) Act 2008, which brought into British law the Lisbon Treaty and its Article 50 procedure, notifying the EU of the UK's intention to leave will supersede the requirements of the European Communities Act 1972 and its later amendments that allow EU law to take precedence over national law. Although the UK would then be able to replace EU law, it would be impractical to strike down all EU law as that could leave a legal void in many areas. What is more, much of the legislation actually originates at the level of United Nations–sponsored bodies, which exist above the European Union.

To avoid this, the complete incorporation of EU legislation, the entire *acquis communautaire* (over 170,000 pages of law), would need to take place via an Act of Parliament. EU law covers most areas of national life. Indeed, the majority of laws and statutory instruments put through national parliaments now come from Brussels. Thus, in 2013 there were in force:

- 8,937 EU Regulations;
- 1,953 EU Directives;
- 15,561 Decisions;
- 2,948 Other Legal Acts;
- 4,733 international agreements;
- 4,843 non-binding legal acts, which may, however, bind if agreed;

- 52,000 agreed EU international standards from CEN, Cenelec, Etsi, etc.;
- 11,961 verdicts from the EU Court of Justice.[11]

There will then be a monumental task for parliament and the civil service of repealing unwelcome EU-inspired rules, while retaining the necessary and acceptable ones.

Will there be a bonfire of the regulations?

It should not be presumed, however, that leaving the EU will necessarily create a significant repeal of laws and regulations. To begin with, the UK's civil service does not favour deregulation. Furthermore, it does not see the regulatory burden as of much of an encumbrance as others, including members of the European Commission. The British Civil Service impact assessments attributed far lower costs to EU regulation than other analyses.

With complex supply chains involved in production, it is difficult to identify, let alone regulate, only a final end point in the production process. In such circumstances, British civil servants may conclude that it is easier to continue applying EU regulation to many sectors of the British economy, especially since the EU will remain Britain's largest trading partner.[12]

Finally, there is plethora of UN-sponsored agencies which produce proposals for legislative standardisation across the world. Thus an increasing amount of what we know as EU legislation actually originates above the EU (North 2013: 10–28). Indeed, the EU recognises such case law as underpinning the workings of the European Union and in this way it becomes, via Brussels, the law of each and every member state. In such circumstances, we will have to be careful not to repeal legislation which originated from

---

11 http://nationalplatform.org/2013/01/12/tackling-the-eueurozones-assault-on -national-democracy/#more-412

12 UK-EU economic relations – key statistics, House of Commons Library, SN/EP/6091, 13 February 2013, page 6.

a UN-sponsored agency to ensure that the UK is not in breach of international standards. This is particularly important as some laws have been developed to avoid non-tariff barriers to trade. At least after Brexit, the UK will have its own voice in these discussions instead of conforming to an agreed EU position, which may not always suit the British national interest. Examples of such bodies are the International Labour Organisation, the World Intellectual Property Organisation and the United Nations Economic Commission for Europe (UNECE). This has several subdivisions including the World Forum for Harmonization of Vehicle Regulations. The WTO, of course, is a further such international body which is a leading player in the international development of standards that remove non-tariff technical barriers to trade. Given the complexities in removing barriers to trade, our membership of the European Economic Area makes sense.

Whereas over 100,000 EU instructions apply to Britain, as of December 2010, only 4,179 EEA relevant acts have been incorporated and are still in force. These 4,179 EEA regulations should be retained, yet they can be modified by the UK. The vast majority of other EU rules can be reviewed when it is practical to do so. In excess of 80 per cent of EEA relevant policy areas fall within the remit of the international standard-setting agencies. Much of the EEA relevant law will be applied after Brexit, regardless of whether the UK retains its membership of the EEA (North 2013: 30). They are a vital part in the process of not only providing standards but also removing technical barriers to trade.

British post-Brexit influence in the EU

There is concern that withdrawing from the European Union will undermine Britain's ability to influence the rules of the UK's most important export market. Not only would Britain have less ability to shape rules that suit British business, but it is feared that we may suffer from Euro-nationalist protectionist measures.

As such, influence needs to be retained. This can be done through the EEA. Norway, an EFTA/EEA, member has actually been described as a 'leader' in EU rule-making. According to the Paris-based Organisation for Economic Cooperation and Development (OECD) – for good or ill – Norway has actually led the EU in formulating environmental legislation.[13] Can the same be said for Britain inside the EU?

EFTA/EEA states sit at the heart of decision-making in Brussels. The difference between them and the EU members is that the EFTA/EEA countries do not have a vote on a regulation or directive at its final stage, in the Council of Ministers, but at that point much has already been decided. The crux of the issue is the weighting attached to each member state's vote in the Council of Ministers: the UK's is small (just around 10 per cent) and so our country can too often be outvoted by a combination of other states.[14]

With its own separate seats and votes, Norway has a far greater global influence in several of the international agencies where all 28 EU member states might have to share just the one EU spot. Norway, in particular, has greater impact in foreign policy by operating free of the EU, so Britain is likely to gain a greater global say by leaving the EU.

If the UK agrees to remain in the EU's customs union, like Turkey, or if a free trade agreement is concluded, then Britain will be told what legislation to adopt as part of the trade deal. However, if Britain retains its membership of the EEA it will have input into the development of Internal Market rules. It will also have

---

13 OECD, Environmental Performance Reviews, Norway 2011.

14 According to *Agreeing to Disagree: The Voting Records of EU Member States in the Council since 2009*, VoteWatch Europe Annual Report 2012, the voting in the Council reflects limited British influence in the EU. From July 2009 to June 2012 Britain voted against the majority more often than any other state; Britain's position has been in the majority on the fewest occasions; Germany votes against Britain more than any other state; and, in the votes that were not unanimous Britain was in the minority on nearly 30 per cent of the votes.

a direct influence on international regulation by partaking as a sovereign state in the UN-sponsored standard setting agencies.

Post-EU trade and migration policy

Post-Brexit, the UK will be able to negotiate trade agreements bilaterally. This has the advantage that it is more likely to achieve the elimination of barriers to British trade. As ever with trade negotiations, there is the difficult issue of whether to remove trade barriers unilaterally. In agriculture, protectionist measures clearly harm consumers. However, in other areas, unilateral action may reduce the possibility that other states and customs unions will reciprocate. Unilateral action also gives the UK less opportunity to influence other states to support the British regulatory environment as there will be little incentive to remove non-technical barriers to exports from the UK.

Being outside the EU customs union, but having tariff-free access, as in the case of the EEA, will be beneficial. It will allow for the unilateral curtailing of tariffs. The UK, if so minded, could cancel or cut the tariff rates charged on imports. Being outside the EU's common external customs levy will enable the prices of many consumer goods to be sold at a lower cost. It will also mean that home-grown producers of, for instance, wine will now face more competition from new world wines, which will then be 32 per cent cheaper. The UK will also have the right to retain the existing tariff system, which the European Union negotiated at the WTO on behalf of the UK, and which currently applies to Britain. The trade schedules will have to be formally approved by the WTO but when this takes place they will be in place upon exit until amended.

Exports to outside the EU make up 60 per cent of total UK exports and this proportion is rising. The EU on the UK's behalf has negotiated preferential trade deals with more than 40 countries outside Europe stretching from Mexico to South Korea. The UK should therefore also seek to retain the EU's existing network of trade agreements. However, it will be possible for the third parties to opt out. According to the Geneva-based Centre for Trade and Economic Integration (Fernekeß et al. 2014),

> ... the third country with whom the agreement has been entered into can terminate it in relation to the UK, based on the termination clause in the treaty or under the rules of international law. Any questions that may arise in this regard can be settled mutually by the parties, or the International Court of Justice.

Furthermore, taking the case of the EU free trade agreement with South Korea, which is regarded as what is known as a 'mixed agreement', the Centre for Trade and Economic Integration have stated that:

> ... the Agreement recognizes the UK as the Contracting Parties to the Treaty on European Union and the Treaty on the Functioning of the European Union. The parties of this agreement are these 'Member States' of the European Union. On withdrawal from the EU, the UK would cease to be a party to the Treaty on European Union and the Treaty on the Functioning of the European Union, which automatically disqualifies it from being a 'party' to the free trade agreement with Korea.

An amicable separation with the EU will therefore be preferable to make sure that the EU supports Britain's continued participation in the free trade agreements and lobbies for the agreements to be amended to accommodate a post-EU Britain. In the UK's exit deal with the EU, a clause will need to be inserted that states that 'the UK is a member of the EU for the purpose of retaining existing international agreements only'. This will enable the numerous international treaties to continue to apply to Britain after the UK leaves what we consider to be the EU. This is of vital importance as these agreements range widely, including the movement of goods and, for example, air passengers. In time they can be renegotiated if necessary and replaced with bilateral agreements between the UK and third-countries but before such a lengthy process can get under way business and consumers will need to know that they will continue. This will require an amicable parting of the ways with the EU and the best way of achieving this will be to remain in the EEA.

A major part of the negotiation of these agreements will have included the promise of levy-free access to the UK's domestic market and since other states around the world will want to keep this it is likely that there will be support for these agreements to be extended to an independent Britain. However, without such an appropriate clause upon Brexit, hundreds of treaties will need to be formally agreed with the states in question.

As well as possible customs levies, UK trade to the continent can be subject to costs from the administrative burden of the EU's customs union. Anything that is already inside the customs union that has originated from a non-member will have been charged at its original port of entry and can therefore circulate freely. At present, as the UK is an EU customs union member, British exporters to the other 27 do not have to prove that they comply with the EU's rules of origin. However, even if the UK had a free trade agreement with the EU, an exporter would have to prove that the goods had been produced, or predominantly worked on, in a state that has a free trade agreement with the EU. If not, the goods will be charged a tariff on its sale price at the applicable rate. As value chains are becoming increasingly globalised, the need to demonstrate an item's origins can be a complex burden.

The Trade Policy Research Centre argues that 'the process of adapting to rules of origin based duty-free trade under a new UK–EU free trade agreement would be tedious, costly and disruptive to trade (Stewart-Brown and Bungay 2012). However, some developments are making this concern less relevant. The reduction in tariffs to zero in many cases reduces the need to complete some of the administrative duties. The EU has also extended the area from which its origin guarantees tariff-free access. This system has already been in existence in the EU and EFTA since 1997 and for Turkey since 1999. From 2017 procedures will be simplified – but will still remain a burden.

Protecting the City of London from EU financial services legislation

For the City of London membership of the European Union is a double-edged sword.

Coming with EU membership is full access to the single-market in services. While this market is far from complete, being part of it, also known as the European Economic Area, is the only way to have full unencumbered access for the sale of services into the EU. The UK's entire financial services sector, which supports an even larger international business services sector, is, however, threatened by the UK's membership of the EU. These businesses sell their services much further afield than the EU, yet inside the European Union they will still be subject to the whims of EU laws proposed by the Commission and agreed by qualified majority vote without the UK having a veto.

EU regulators, the European Banking Authority, the European Insurance and Occupational Pensions Authority and the European Securities Authority have been established to regulate and standardise regulations across the EU. The European Systemic Risk Council and the European System of Financial Supervisors control will have the power to close down a financial institution. The EU bureaucracy has already begun interfering in UK financial institutions.

In general, financial services companies are internationally mobile, as are the business services companies that support financial services, and now generate a high proportion of UK exports. They are also one of the most productive parts of the UK economy. However, this is threatened by the growth of EU regulation. The UK must follow a path that will both protect businesses from the harmful effects of EU regulators while preserving full access to the Single Market. What can be done to achieve this?

Firstly, there is the example of Switzerland, which like Britain has a strong financial services industry. Although the Swiss have a series of free trade agreements in goods, these do not cover the export of services. Swiss-based companies do not have the right to sell their services to the EU unless they establish a subsidiary inside the European Economic Area.

There is another way. The UK can leave the EU, freeing businesses from the European Commission's quangos, and keep full access to the Single Market. The only way this can be achieved is for Britain to rejoin the successful and non-authoritarian European Free Trade Association (EFTA) and thus remain a member of the European Economic Area (EEA), also known as the Single Market.

Aligning the UK with EFTA will at a stroke free Britain's financial services industry from control by:

- The EBA (European Banking Authority).
- The European Insurance and Occupational Pensions Authority.
- The European Systemic Risk Board.
- The European Securities and Markets Authority (ESMA).
- The Community Programme for Financial Reporting and Auditing.

EFTA/EEA nations are also free from European Union tax law including the EU Financial Transaction Tax. As a member of EFTA, Britain will also be able to veto the regulations that threaten pay within the financial services sector, such as 'Recommendation on remuneration in the financial sector 32009H0384'.

Foreign direct investment

The UK is the leading destination for foreign direct investment (FDI) in the European Union. How will Brexit affect this investment?

While investment decisions are based on more important factors than belonging to a political union – such as the host country's tax regime and the opportunity for economic growth – the ability to easily access as large a market as possible will undoubtedly be a consideration. According to a survey by Ernst & Young (2013), 56 per cent of investors from Western Europe thought that less integration would harm investment into the UK and only 38 per cent thought that it would make Britain more attractive. However, 72 per cent of companies interviewed in North America thought reduced integration into the EU would make the UK more attractive as an FDI location and two-thirds of Asian respondents thought that a lower degree of EU integration would make the UK a more attractive location for FDI. Thus, EU integration may be retarding UK economic activity and it is even conceivable that investment in Britain will increase if the UK remains in the less integration EEA alternative.

Does admission to a large base of consumers encourage FDI? There is research which suggests that it does. A survey by Nigel Pain of the OECD and Garry Young of the Bank of England concluded that exit from the EU could cost the UK as much as 2¼ per cent of GDP primarily from lost FDI (Pain et al. 2004). Does this mean that nations in the EU exponentially benefit from foreign investment and nations outside suffer from a dearth of FDI? In fact, evidence from UNSTAD shows that it is the EU that is suffering from a shortage of FDI. In terms of FDI counted in US dollars ($) per capita, it is clear that membership of EFTA benefits its members far more than belonging to the EU (see Table 13).[15]

---

15 http://unctadstat.unctad.org/TableViewer/tableView.aspx

Table 13   Foreign direct investment flows per capita per year (US $)

Year	2001	2002	2003	2004	2005	2006	2007	2008	2009	2010	2011
Economy											
EFTA	926	591	1,666	342		348	4,657	3,754	2,072	3,562	3,845	2,397
EU27	796	647	584	464	1,019	1,182	1,730	1,093	717	755	876
Euro zone	922	792	738	420	795	1,055	1,691	1,103	734	942	1,004
UK	906	422	458	950	2,944	2,570	3,272	1,447	1,233	813	816

Figure 4 makes a comparison of the stock of FDI for Iceland, Switzerland, Norway (members of the European Free Trade Association) and the UK. The trend is clear. The three independent EFTA countries drew markedly ahead in 1993, and then established a clear lead from 2001, which continued to widen

Figure 4   FDI in Iceland, Switzerland, Norway in comparison with the UK (1983–2012), Central Bank of Iceland (1989–2012)

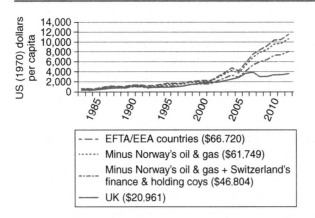

--- EFTA/EEA countries ($66.720)

...... Minus Norway's oil & gas ($61,749)

_.._ Minus Norway's oil & gas + Switzerland's finance & holding coys ($46,804)

——— UK ($20,961)

Sources: UNCTADstat Foreign direct investment stocks and flows, annual, 1970–2012. http://unctadstat.unctad.org/UnctadStatMetadata/Classifications/Tables&Indicators.html
OECDstat Dataset: Foreign direct investment: positions by industry, Reporting country Norway.
WTO, Trade Policy Review: Switzerland and Liechtenstein, Table 1.4 Foreign direct investment, 2008–11, 23 April 2013: http://www.wto.org/english/thewto_e/countries_e/switzerland_e.htm (http://statistics.cb.is/en/data/set/).

thereafter. From 2005 their FDI stock increased at a much more rapid rate, and continued to do so even through the financial crisis. To avoid any distortion caused through Norway's oil and gas industry and Switzerland's financial services, this FDI relating to those industries has been removed. Still, the figures show that the EEA/EFTA states achieve higher levels of FDI outside the EU. The UK should seek to replicate the high levels of FDI which those states regularly achieve.

Just as it is clear that belonging to the EU's political union may be detrimental to FDI, access to a large market, as the EFTA states have, is clearly important.

Post-EU immigration policy – and the rights of British citizens to reside in the EU

Though there is much discussion about migration from the rest of the EU to the UK, 1.8 million UK citizens live in other EU states. They take advantage of the free movement of persons – a right enshrined in EU treaties. Those that have established a residency, which will include both living and owning property, in an EU member state will have their rights protected upon withdrawal.

This entitlement is known as an 'executed right'. Article 70 b. of the Vienna Convention states that the withdrawal from a treaty 'Does not affect any right, obligation or legal situation of the parties created through the execution of the treaty prior to its termination.' This view is supported by the constitutional expert Lord McNair. He concluded that such rights established by a treaty will remain in force even if the agreement is terminated by Britain's exit. In law they are considered to be executed by the treaty and 'have an existence independent of it; the termination cannot touch them.' Their status will be guaranteed as a result of the 'well-recognised principle of respect for acquired [vested] rights' (McNair 1961). Furthermore, it is a legal norm and the Oxford Journal in its year book on international law argues that Acquired Rights are

Customary Law and therefore take precedence over national law at the international level. Furthermore, they will be regarded as such by the International Court of Justice in the Hague.

Therefore the impact of Britain leaving the EU will not be that great for those EU citizens already resident here or for British citizens living abroad. The difference will be felt by those who move to a different state after British withdrawal.

Indeed, cancelling the right to live and work of French and German citizens already in the UK would need separate legislation and presumably prove to be diplomatically contentious. London is now the fourth largest 'French city'. According to a November 2013 report by the Centre for Research and Analysis Migration (Dustmann and Frattini 2013), between 2001 and 2011 immigrants to the UK from the EEA contributed 34 per cent more in taxes than the British state spent on supporting them.

For the future, however, it is possible to impose restrictions on immigration while remaining in the EEA. Liechtenstein, an EEA member with less potential influence than Britain, continues to use clauses in the EEA agreement to restrict the movement of persons. Article 112(1) of the EEA Agreement reads: 'If serious economic, societal or environmental difficulties of a sectorial or regional nature liable to persist are arising, a Contracting Party may unilaterally take appropriate measures under the conditions and procedures laid down in Article 113.' The restrictions used by Liechtenstein are further reinforced by Protocol 15 (Articles 5–7) of the EEA agreement. This allows Liechtenstein to keep specific restrictions on the free movement of people. These have been kept in place by what is known as the EEA Council.[16]

The restrictions that the UK government should impose would focus on those from the EU nations that are in receipt of EEA grants. Citizens of those states should be subject to work

---

16 EEA Council Decision No. 1/95, Official Journal of the European Communities, 20 April 1995, pages L 86/58 and 86/80.

permits. This is in line with the stated policy of the prime minister to restrict immigration from the less-well-off states in the EU. There is every reason to believe that this policy can be delivered through an EEA agreement.[17,18]

As members of the EEA, the UK should in time seek to develop appropriate policies for migration and work permits for the 16 less-well-off EEA states. It should be noted that even when controls were placed on Bulgarian citizens, the UK never refused a work permit request from Bulgaria after that nation's accession to the EU.

There will also be greater latitude to restrict non-British EU citizens' access to benefits and to deny residency to those who are deemed to not have sufficient resources to support themselves. The current debate in Britain on immigration largely ignores the role of the European Court of Human Rights and the European Convention.

Article 3 of the Convention (inhuman or degrading treatment or punishment) and Article 8 (private and family life, his home and his correspondence) would also be relevant to the issue of immigration. These two articles are often taken together, especially in cases of repatriation.

EEA/EFTA states are outside Article 6 of the EU's Treaty on European Union, which states:

> 2. The Union shall accede to the European Convention for the Protection of Human Rights and Fundamental Freedoms. Such accession shall not affect the Union's competences as defined in the Treaties.

---

17 http://www.telegraph.co.uk/news/uknews/immigration/10517128/Stop
-unrestricted-immigration-from-poor-EU-countries-David-Cameron-suggests
.html

18 http://www.telegraph.co.uk/news/newstopics/eureferendum/11141331/Iain
-Duncan-Smith-cut-migration-or-Britain-could-quit-EU.html

3. Fundamental rights, as guaranteed by the European Convention for the Protection of Human Rights and Fundamental Freedoms and as they result from the constitutional traditions common to the Member States, shall constitute general principles of the Union's law.

Alternatives to the EU

The European Free Trade Association

Since the UK left EFTA the remaining member states have prospered more than EU members. With an average unemployment rate of just 4 per cent, EFTA is one of the most effective trading associations in the world. Despite consisting of the relatively small states of Iceland, Norway and Switzerland, and the micro-state of Liechtenstein, it still has considerable trade with the EU – with exports of more than €189.2 billion a year. That is nearly as much as the US, which exported just over €190 billion worth of goods to the EU in 2011. That same year, EFTA states sold more than €102 billion worth of services to the EU – more than China, Russia and Japan combined (EFTA 2013, Figure 9).

Certainly, the EFTA model of free trade without political interference or over-regulation is beneficial. The rules governing EFTA, known as the 'EFTA Convention', cover just 30 pages. The EU's combined Treaty on European Union and Treaty on the Functioning of the European Union totals 186 pages.

The balance sheet of costs to the taxpayer is also telling. Whereas EFTA's 2013 budget amounted to no more than £15.6 million, the EU spends some €7 billion on administration each year. Further, whereas the EU's accounts have not received the approval of its own Court of Auditors for the past 20 years – concluding that they remain subject to waste, mismanagement and fraud – EFTA's accounts are approved and signed off each year without qualification. While the European Commission, which is divorced from national democratic oversight, manages the EU's budget, EFTA's finances are administered by a Budget Committee which is part of the EFTA Council.

EFTA has its head office in Geneva, Switzerland, with 80 staff working in its Secretariat compared with 30,000 in the EU bureaucracy. Indeed, EFTA is simply an intergovernmental organisation primarily engaged in negotiating trade agreements with both EU and non-EU countries. Unlike the EU, it is neither a supranational political bureaucracy nor a customs union controlling the trade policy of member states.

The EFTA Council, which usually meets twice a year, manages relations between the EFTA states under the terms of the EFTA Convention. Through this intergovernmental council the member states can consult, negotiate and act together, as well as develop their links with other countries and trade groups around the world. The attendees at its meetings are usually relevant ministers from its member states. Extra meetings are usually attended by the member states' ambassadors to the European Free Trade Association.

EFTA also has representation in Brussels providing support for the running of relations with the European Union under what is known as the European Economic Area Agreement and assists member states to prepare for and to implement new legislation as part of the EFTA members' treaty with the contracting parties from the EU. There is also an EFTA Statistical Office contributing to Eurostat. This is another important mechanism by which EFTA can and does influence the development of EU rules by taking part in EU technical meetings and other EU committees. The opinions of experts from the EFTA countries do matter. In fact, EFTA and the EU have good working relations. The opinions of the representatives from the more prosperous EFTA countries are valued in discussions with their EU counterparts. EFTA is also actively involved in negotiating with the UN-sponsored standardisation agencies.

Unlike the EU, EFTA does not involve itself in countries' agriculture, fisheries, home affairs or justice policies. It concluded a free trade agreement with South Korea that came into force on 1 September 2006 – five years before one secured by the EU. EFTA has free trade with 36 countries outside the EU. Indeed, over 80 per cent of its trade in goods is with states with which it has negotiated preferential trade arrangements. Unlike EU states, EFTA members are free to negotiate their own free trade agreements with any other country. On 15 April 2013 Iceland signed one with China – the first FTA the Chinese have had with a European country. Switzerland followed, signing a free trade agreement with the Chinese on 6 July 2013.[19] Clearly, it is a misconception that only large political and economic blocs can pull off such important agreements.

Membership of EFTA allows its member states to take advantage of its network and to develop its own trade agreements. Considerable benefit can be obtained from Britain concluding its own trade agreements. The expansion in trade by the Swiss shows what can be achieved and this contrasts with the inadequate results of the trade agreements negotiated on Britain's behalf by the EU.

If we analyse the 15 countries with which EU free trade agreements were struck between 1992 and 2008, it is notable that, while in six of the countries the annual average rate of growth of UK exports increased, in seven it declined and in two it remained the same. The increases in trade tended to be with the countries with which the UK does less trade. This contrasts with Switzerland, which has increased trade with nearly all the 14 countries with which it has struck free trade agreements. This may well be because, when out of the EU, countries can more effectively identify the partners with which they prioritise free trade agreements,

---

19 https://www.ige.ch/fileadmin/user_upload/Juristische_Infos/e/Switzerland_China_FTA_Main_Agreement.pdf

but it is also because the Swiss were able to include services and target larger markets. Aligning with the Swiss through EFTA will therefore be useful.

It can therefore be concluded that British exports will increase after Brexit through expanding bilateral free trade agreements.

EFTA/EEA membership has also encouraged trade with the Single Market. Once EFTA states were granted full access to the internal market in 1992, they enjoyed rapid export growth, which now exceeds the rate of increase from the UK in exports from the UK to the other Single Market countries. This reflects the increasingly international supply chains in both agricultural and industrial goods. EFTA takes a liberal approach to the origins of imports. If the item in question has been either 'wholly obtained' or 'sufficiently worked or processed' in a state that has signed a free trade agreement with EFTA, then it can be imported without difficulty. Any disputes that arise in EFTA are resolved through a system of arbitration – not by diktat from the European Commission or European Court of Justice.

Rejoining EFTA makes sense on both economic and political grounds. It allows the UK a formal role in EU/EEA discussions and is also likely to prove popular with the British public. A recent Survation opinion poll for the Bruges Group found that 71 per cent of respondents favoured the EFTA alternative, with just 29 per cent wanting to remain in the European Union.[20]

The UK is considered to be a member of the EEA as the EEA's founding treaty states that a nation can be a member of either the EU or EFTA. Belonging to either one of those will enable the continuation, without let or hindrance, of the free movement of goods, services, capital and labour into the EU's Single Market. The EEA Agreement is flexible. Unlike the convoluted process

---

20 http://www.brugesgroup.com/eu/71-said-they-would-prefer-britain-to-leave-the
-eu-and-join-efta.htm?xp=comment

of treaty change in the EU it remains easy and incumbent upon the EEA Council to amend the agreement. Article 89 says that the EEA Council 'shall assess the overall functioning and the development of the Agreement. It shall take the political decisions leading to amendments of the Agreement.' What is more, the European Commission believes that the EEA is due for reform; the continued participation of the UK if it were out of the EU could provide the impetus for changing the agreement.

Beyond guaranteeing full access to the Single Market, what else does continued membership of the EEA have to offer?

The Norwegian option: the European Economic Area

In 1992 three EFTA states, Iceland, Liechtenstein and Norway, elected to take part in the Single Market without becoming members of the EU. This is the so-called 'Norway option'. The EEA agreement was seen as a way of expanding access to the Single Market to EFTA members without having to dilute the goal of ever-closer union. The arrangement is straightforward and its first article stipulates:

... the association shall entail, in accordance with the provisions of this Agreement:

(a) the free movement of goods;

(b) the free movement of persons (this however is qualified and limited, furthermore opt-outs exist);

(c) the free movement of services;

(d) the free movement of capital;

(e) the setting up of a system ensuring that competition is not distorted and that the rules thereon are equally respected; as well as

(f) closer cooperation in other fields, such as research and development, the environment, education and social policy.

If the much-vaunted potential free trade deal between the US and the EU, the Transatlantic Trade and Investment Partnership (TTIP), is agreed it will also cover the EEA states. This will give Iceland, Liechtenstein and Norway tariff-free access to the US economy. Britain could therefore benefit from this without remaining in the EU and remain at the forefront of TTIP negotiations. This is important because, otherwise, international regulations under US/EU leadership might by disadvantageous to our interests. If other states join with the UK in EFTA, then the axis of TTIP can be changed from a predominantly bipartisan EU/US basis to the tripartite EU/EFTA/US and ultimately to a quartet of the EU/EFTA/US and the Commonwealth.

As an EEA member the mutual recognition of standards would continue to apply to British exporters wanting to sell their goods to other EU and EEA states. If approved in one member state, a product could be sold in another without having to undergo new testing to see if it complies with the regulations of the country to which it is being exported. The agreement that establishes the European Economic Area assures 'equal rights and obligations within the Single Market for citizens and economic operators in the EEA.'[21]

The obligations which come with EEA membership include the requirement to make grants to less well-off countries in the EEA. These payments do not go directly into the EU's funds. The financial contributions made to the EEA programmes, known as EEA and Norway Grants, go towards reducing inequality among its 30 members. They are targeted at the 16 least prosperous EEA states: the 12 that have joined since 2004 as well as the impoverished Greece, Portugal and Spain. Iceland, Liechtenstein and Norway also participate in numerous EU programmes, ranging from culture to transport and lifelong learning in the EU, many of which are optional. This gives the EEA states influence but there

---

21 Free Trade Agreements, *This is EFTA 2013*, European Free Trade Association, 2013.

is a cost. A House of Commons report found that, in 2011, the total cost for Norway of these programmes came to £524 million – £106 per head of population compared with gross payments by the UK to the EU of £243 per capita per annum.

The benefits of the Norway option are not just financial. Unlike the EU, EEA membership preserves national sovereignty in a number of important areas, including justice and home affairs, foreign policy, tax policies, agriculture and control of fishing grounds. Members are outside the EU's customs union and free to make their own trade agreements. While it is true that Iceland, Liechtenstein and Norway are obliged to implement some EU rules, these countries adopt 70 per cent fewer regulations than those imposed on EU member states. While neither Norwegian ministers nor parliamentarians can attend or vote in the meetings of the Council of Ministers, or in the European Parliament, they have the right not only to be consulted about EU rules but can also shape EU decisions at the start. Indeed, EEA representatives take part in more than 500 EU committees and expert groups.

The management of the EEA agreement is also not top down from the European Union. The EFTA Surveillance Authority monitors whether or not free competition is being followed and that markets are open to business from EU members. Any contravention of the rules by a member state or company can be reported to the Court of Justice of the European Free Trade Association States, which has jurisdiction to interpret the EEA agreement. Unlike the EU's ECJ, which can overrule and strike down national law, the EFTA Court can only state that a national law is incompatible with the EEA agreement. Resolution can only come from national institutions – not through the EEA and EFTA institutions. What is more, disputes are resolved at a political intergovernmental level, not by judges or bureaucrats in the Commission exercising their power in a supranational institution. Ultimately, for the EFTA/EEA states, it is for the national government to decide how a breach of the EEA agreement can best be remedied.

When EFTA countries choose to adopt EU rules, they do not do so as countries that have transferred the making of legislation to the EU as Britain has. Nations such as Norway establish EEA-relevant rules at the national level. The legislation is not directly imposed from above by the EU. Furthermore, the EFTA states that have agreed to be part of the EEA can opt out of areas of EEA where they feel that legislation does not serve their national interest. Inside the EU, the UK does not have this right.[22]

Implementation of those acts that are not vetoed or ignored are often delayed by Norway. The custom of the EFTA states being responsible for drafting the decision of the EEA Joint Committee often allows them to delay their implementation. The delaying of the translation of EEA-relevant decisions into Norwegian dialects is also regularly used to postpone implementation. Those EEA-relevant acts that are not delayed are often altered. The EFTA/EEA states demand that more than a third of the acts, and as many of 40 per cent of those which deal with services, are changed. This is not just an opportunity to tailor EEA rules to the EFTA states' advantage; it is also in itself yet another source of delay: negotiations then ensue. This is certainly not fax democracy.[23]

The EEA agreement is business friendly. It allows for investor country disputes to be raised and discussed by the EFTA Surveillance Authority and the EFTA Court. WTO challenges are limited to just country versus country disputes.

Certainly, there are costs associated with the EEA but with Britain as a member of both EFTA and the EEA there could be a change in the relationship between Brussels and the two organisations. Presumably Britain, in partnership with the current EFTA states, would fight for lower EEA grants to the less-well-off

---

22 Article 102, *Agreement on the European Economic Area* (OJ No L 1, 3.1.1994, p. 3; and EFTA States' official gazettes).

23 Commission Staff Working document: a review of the functioning of the European Economic Area, Brussels, 12 December 2012, 17626/12.

states, for more influence in the development of EU law, fewer areas where EU standards apply and for restoring the original principle of co-decision between independent EFTA countries and the EU. This may well be achievable. The European Commission itself acknowledges that, if the European Economic Area agreement is updated membership of it 'would offer EEA EFTA countries a convenient "alternative EU Membership-status on an à la carte basis".[24]

This is essentially British policy: access to the Single Market while having the right to reject rules that are not in the national interest. But it would be achieved from without, rather than from within the EU via the present approach of seeking an implausible renegotiation to achieve the same objectives. Alternatively, the UK could attempt to follow the path of another European state that has rejected the EEA model of pan-European economic co-operation. This nation is Switzerland.

The Swiss option: EFTA without the EEA

Switzerland is a member of EFTA but not of the EEA. Yet Switzerland still has full access to the Single Market. They achieve this through free trade agreements and have observer status in the formal EFTA/EEA structure.

In fact, Switzerland has about 120 bilateral trade arrangements with the EU, the main body of which was concluded in 1999. The Swiss refer to them as Bilaterals I. The agreements liberalise trade in areas ranging from agriculture to air and land transport. To allow for easier trade they also standardise technical rules and allow for access to the public procurement market. Through this 1999 agreement, Switzerland also partakes in the EU's research programmes. The free movement of people is also part of Bilaterals I. The recent Swiss rejection of the movement

---

24 Ibid.

of free people will, however, bring this whole set of agreements into doubt and may lead to their cancellation. There is an FTA on industrial goods dating from 1972 which abolished quotas and customs duties, but not customs checks. There was also a 1989 agreement on companies being able to establish insurance services in each other's territory.

In 2004 Switzerland and the EU reached a further accord with Brussels known as Bilaterals II. They have chosen to enhance their cooperation with the EU in areas where they consider that mutual benefit can be obtained. Switzerland also opted to become a member of the Schengen agreement, which eliminated border controls between the participating states. Britain and Ireland are not members of this, choosing to stay out.

The 2004 agreement also covers rights for asylum seekers. The Swiss ratified the so-called Dublin Regulation (2003/343/CE) on refugees in a referendum in 2005. It also covers pensions, information on the taxation of savings, measures to fight fraud, participation in the EU's media activities, and an agreement on the environment whereby Switzerland comes under the umbrella of the EU's Environment Agency. The participation in the EU's statistical programme is included in this agreement. The Swiss became involved with Europol and in 2008 they joined Eurojust; these two measures encourage police and judicial cooperation between the EU and Switzerland. In 2010 they opted to take part in EU youth, educational and training programmes.

Switzerland adopts fewer EU rules than EEA members such as Norway; but the Norwegians, via the formal structure of the EEA, have greater input into the development of EU law.

Switzerland is not totally without a voice. There are fifteen joint committees made up of representatives from the European Commission's directorate for trade with neighbouring countries and from Switzerland's government. They meet to discuss issues that arise out of their FTAs, including rules of origin relating to products from outside the customs union coming into the EU via Switzerland, and vice versa. They also discuss the possibility of imposing EU rules on the confederation. While there does have to be mutual agreement before EU rules are applied, the Commission does have the advantage in negotiations. The economic dominance of the EU's internal market and the common right to cancel the agreements in the event of non-compliance makes Switzerland the junior partner. In some ways, the Swiss arrangement is beginning to almost resemble the relationship that Norway has via the EEA but without the formalised input mechanisms that Norway has into the development of EEA-relevant rules.

Most of the Swiss trade agreements with the EU have taken up to seven years to negotiate. Whereas Swiss–EU relations have been built on an already existing FTA, apart from membership of the EEA, the UK has nothing that could form the basis of a free trade agreement with the EU. Furthermore, Brexit could be a geopolitical shock to the EU that may foster resentment and a fear that others will also leave the fold.

Whereas the Swiss are mostly happy with their highly complex EU arrangements, the EU is not. The EU would prefer a system where Single Market–relevant rules are adopted automatically rather than the proliferation of committees that can legally ignore them. This, however, rarely happens. The EU's experience will make them reluctant to enter into precisely the same arrangement with Britain.

Furthermore, while the EU is mandated to reach trade agreements with its neighbours, it is unlikely that the complex issues surrounding the UK's post-EU membership trade would be resolved quickly. Given the uncertainty of having to wait until non-tariff trade arrangements and freedom of movement of capital and services are agreed, the clock will probably rule out the Swiss model as a viable option.

The Swiss are again facing pressure from the EU to change their relationship with Brussels so that they conform more automatically to EU standards and they are currently resisting. One reason why the EU may not wish to agree to the so-called Swiss option being applied to the UK is that it will bolster the Swiss case for refusing to alter their bilateral agreements. Other countries have taken yet another course to gain access to the Single Market without belonging to the EEA or negotiating complex trade agreements. This is the option of remaining in the EU's customs union.

The Turkish option: remaining in the customs union

Turkey's membership of the customs union was completed on 31 December 1995. Along with EU members, Turkey is part of the trade alliance that allows it to export goods to the EU without paying the EU's external tariff, which applies to imports from outside the customs union. This access applies for all produce except non-processed agricultural goods. The EU's public procurement and service markets are also closed to Turkish-based companies.

Turkey has had to adopt some EU law, particularly in the area of industrial standards. Although it is a member of the Euro–Mediterranean partnership, it has little effective input into the formulation of the rules the EU asks it to apply. Furthermore, Article 8 of the customs union agreement gives the EU influence over Turkish law. It states, 'Turkey shall incorporate into its internal legal order the Community instruments relating to the removal of technical barriers to trade.' This especially relates to EU 'instruments deemed to be of particular importance.' Further, Article 66 mandates that the agreement must conform to the rulings of the European Court of Justice – a body on which Turkey has no representation.[25]

---

25 http://www.avrupa.info.tr/fileadmin/Content/Downloads/PDF/Custom_Union_des_ENG.pdf

Tellingly, the agreement with Turkey, at 61 pages, is more than twice the length of the EEA agreement. What is more, the Turkish government now finds the agreement objectionable and wants it changed. The Turkish Economy Minister, Nihat Zeybekci, stated to business leaders on 23 March 2014 that his government wanted to renegotiate the agreement 'to which no sovereign independent state should agree.' A particular problem was caused through the EU entering into free trade agreements with third-countries whose producers could then export goods into Turkey tariff-free without them having to grant reciprocal access to Turkish products.[26]

Other states that are out of the EU's immediate orbit but belong to the customs union are San Marino, Monaco and Andorra. The Principality of the Valleys of Andorra, like Turkey, has agricultural products excluded from the agreement while the other microstates do not.

If Britain left the EU it would have to negotiate to remain in the customs union. While other non-EU parties to EU trade agreements will give their acquiescence, as Britain was part of the deal when the trade links were established, it is by no means certain that the EU will consent. The EU is not a rational economic actor. Furthermore, remaining in the customs union will mean that the EU's external tariff would continue to apply to imports to the UK. However, under this alternative, anti-dumping action can then be taken against British exporters as it can be in theory against those from Turkey. The European Commission would ultimately still determine the UK's trade policy. Furthermore, it would mean that the UK would not be able to negotiate its own new trade agreements or take advantage of opportunities in emerging world markets unless it had the consent of the EU.

Britain is already a member of the EEA and can keep this status with little practical difficulty. Attaining just membership of

---

26 http://www.neurope.eu/article/turkey-wants-renegotiate-eu-customs-union

the customs union will require negotiation. The EEA is the safer option as such a status can be routinely achieved.

No agreement

There exists the possibility that there will not be an accord between Britain and the EU upon Brexit. A free trade deal may not be completed and either Britain's application to EFTA may be rejected or the UK could choose not to join the EEA. In this scenario, tariffs would have to be applied against Britain.

The World Trade Organization would protect Britain's right to export to the remaining EU states and go part of the way to safeguarding the UK's interests. Yet, there are still parts of the British economy – for example, the automotive industry – that would be seriously disadvantaged by levies placed on imports to the continent. Customs duties remain significant in some areas and not just on motor vehicles. The EU's average most favoured nation on agricultural produce is 13.2 per cent and 4.2 per cent on non-agricultural goods.[27]

Could Britain mitigate those costs? Subsidies to meet export targets are prohibited under World Trade Organization rules and such an approach runs the risk of provoking a complaint to the WTO and allowing the EU to take countermeasures on British products such as anti-dumping actions.

Future trade alliances should better reflect Britain's interests and world outlook. Where nations have similar economic interests they are more likely to seek mutually beneficial trade policies. This is a more rational approach to international trade relations than simply aligning with the nearest geopolitical bloc. However, forming new agreements will be a time-consuming process. What is more, there are significant countries in an already existing association that have remarkable similarities to Britain: Norway and

---

27 http://stat.wto.org/TariffProfiles/E27_E.htm

Switzerland, the two main states in EFTA. Both share with the UK a similar liberal-democratic culture as well as economic complementarities. Norwegian economic success is built on chemicals, fishing and the extraction of both gas and oil. Switzerland has strengths that include biotechnology, engineering, finance and pharmaceuticals. These are all strengths from which the British economy benefits. As such, the UK should try to join EFTA.

The process of rejoining EFTA

Should the UK wish to do so, applying for EFTA membership is straightforward and is contained within Article 56 of the EFTA Convention. The key point reads: 'Any State may accede to this Convention, provided that the Council decides to approve its accession, on such terms and conditions as may be set out in that decision.'

There are also other forms of relationship with EFTA. As the Convention states: 'The Council may negotiate an agreement between the Member States and any other State, union of States or international organisation, creating an association embodying such reciprocal rights and obligations, common actions and special procedures as may be appropriate. Such an agreement shall be submitted to the Member States for acceptance and shall enter into force provided that it is accepted by all Member States.' EFTA's substantial trade network can be accessed via section 3: 'Any State acceding to this Convention shall apply to become a party to the free trade agreements between the Member States on the one hand and third states, unions of states or international organisations on the other.'[28]

The UK should apply to join EFTA as soon as the Article 50 notice to the EU has been given. Its EFTA membership will not

28 http://www.efta.int/sites/default/files/documents/legal-texts/efta-convention/ Vaduz%20Convention%20Agreement.pdf

become live until it is outside the EU – until that time the UK can have observer status making it a de facto member, with the ability to help shape its development.

Reforming the EEA and EFTA: re-establishing the original purpose of the EEA

As far as the 'other Europeans' are concerned, the question is quite simple: how do we reconcile the successful integration of the Twelve without rebuffing those who are just as entitled to call themselves Europeans?

... we can look for a new, more structured partnership with common decision-making and administrative institutions to make our activities more effective and to highlight the political dimension of our cooperation in the economic, social, financial and cultural spheres.

Jacques Delors, 17 January 1989 (in EFTA 2009),
President of the European Commission Strasbourg,

Delors understood that Europe was more than the EU. He also wanted to grant trade access to those who did not want to take part in political union. A key part of the access to the planned Single Market was to be co-decision on EEA-relevant regulation between the EU and the EFTA states. These laudable aims were, however, later abandoned. Due to a number of countries leaving EFTA the EEA did not develop as an equal partnership between the EU and EFTA. Expanding EFTA can restore this balance.

The workings of the EEA institutions are arguably more transparent than the fifteen behind-closed-doors meetings of the EU–Swiss joint commissions on trade. There is already a great deal of flexibility in the EEA agreement. This goes beyond the ability to restrict immigration and opt-out of areas of EEA rules.

Iceland even unilaterally imposed capital controls after its financial crash in 2008. This is permitted within the EEA safeguards Article 112.[29] There is also no enforcement mechanism to prevent this from happening even if such flexibility was not contained within the EEA. While this paper does not advocate such a policy, it shows that radical steps that run contrary, even to the four freedoms of the EEA, can be implemented. The EEA-relevant rule relating to freedom of movement, Directive 2004/38, has qualifications, conditions and limitations. These include:

(10) Persons exercising their right of residence should not, however, become an unreasonable burden on the social assistance system of the host Member State during an initial period of residence. Therefore, the right of residence for Union citizens and their family members for periods in excess of three months should be subject to conditions.

(12) For periods of residence of longer than three months, Member States should have the possibility to require Union citizens to register with the competent authorities in the place of residence, attested by a registration certificate issued to that effect.

(22) The Treaty allows restrictions to be placed on the right of free movement and residence on grounds of public policy, public security or public health.

Article 7 (1)
(b) have sufficient resources for themselves and their family members not to become a burden on the social assistance system of the host Member State during their period of residence

---

29 Official Journal of the European Communities, 3 January 1994, pages L/28, 176-8 and 562.

and have comprehensive sickness insurance cover in the host
Member State.[30]

No right is absolute, and neither is freedom of movement within the EEA. What is more, EEA rules only apply to EFTA nations
after they have assessed the relevant legislation and applied it
according to their own interpretation of what freedom of movement means.

Can Britain inspire reforms in the EEA so that it better suits
the UK's needs? Much can be done unilaterally. As an EEA member outside the EU, the UK will also have the ability to rewrite
EEA-relevant rules. While they must still broadly conform to
existing legislation it will grant some latitude to make sure that
British interests are better served.

Britain will have considerable influence in EFTA. Indeed, it
can use its considerable negotiating power to make sure that its
agenda is considered by both EFTA and the EEA Council which
can change the EEA agreement.

What is more, the UK will not be alone. Through remaining
in the EEA and rejoining EFTA, the UK will acquire allies that
can negotiate alongside the UK. Bilateral negotiations between
the UK and the 27 other remaining EU states supported by the
European Commission and the pro-centralisation European
Parliament puts the UK at a disadvantage. Within the EEA, the
UK will gain Switzerland as an ally. The Swiss have a reputation
as tough negotiators; their involvement on our side will act as a
force multiplier.

The EFTA Secretariat recognises that an expanded EFTA can
change the balance of power in Europe:

---

30 Directive 2004/38/EC of the European Parliament and of the Council of 29 April
2004.

Increasing the number of EFTA members would reinvigorate the tradition of a common platform of negotiations with the European Union and other countries … The increase in membership would reinforce the standing of EFTA vis-à-vis the European Union, within the WTO and with other international organisations. An extended membership would also increase the potential for concluding substantial FTAs with third countries and for finding solutions in latching on appropriately to future systems of preferential trade, encompassing major markets.

Professor Thomas Cottier, of the University of Bern, argues that the original reason for EFTA was to offer a joint platform for negotiations with the EEC. This will be restored if Britain rejoins EFTA.

According to EFTA, it could, '… develop into an institutional host for existing and future EU association with states wishing to maintain the traditional perceptions of national sovereignty within Europe.'[31]

Britain will be much better off in a reformed EFTA/EEA arrangement where the members of this EU-out group have perhaps more autonomy from Single Market legislation rule making and/or more influence over its formulation. The flexibility of the EEA and an organically evolving relationship will be preferable in the short term to a trade deal which has fixed terms applying to the UK.

With a reformed relationship in place it may, in the long term, be desirable to replace or cancel the EEA agreement. In the short-to-medium term the UK will have led in the formulation of 'EFTA plus'. This would be a further empowered EFTA with an improved relationship with the EU and an expanded network of trade links abroad cooperating with the Commonwealth. What

---

31 EFTA Bulletin, EFTA Free Trade Relations, December 2013.

is more, the Commonwealth states traditionally supported the UK's lead in the formation of EFTA as it would strengthen Britain as a market for their goods (Attwood 1961).

When Lord Lawson, Chancellor of the Exchequer 1983–89, announced that he favoured withdrawal from the EU, he estimated that any loss of trade to the EU's Single Market could be made good by increasing sales to the rest of the world.[32] Under the EFTA/EEA alternative there is no reason to believe that trade with the remaining EU states will diminish yet the UK will, for the first time since 1973, be able to explore real opportunities overseas.

Gateway UK: linking the Commonwealth and the EEA

If Britain retains tariff-free access to the Single Market and develops trade links with third-country states, it will allow the UK to take advantage of the growth in global value chains. A more liberal regulatory regime and tariff-free access to the Single Market will make the UK a base by which third-country producers that have entered preferential trade deals with Britain can access the EU without being subject to tariffs and they will be less likely to face anti-dumping.

This will require some degree of reworking and/or final assembly of goods within the UK. Within Britain value can be added to goods and re-exported from the UK to the Single Market. This will allow exporters to sidestep the EU's rules-of-origin regime. Britain will be able to become a regional value-added production hub. The British economy will therefore not only benefit from the additional bilateral trade with other territories but will also capture a number of benefits such as increased freight and haulage and increased assembly and manufacturing

---

32 Lawson, Lord Nigel, *The Times*, 7 May 2013.

within the UK (to meet rules of origin that require a declaration to be made that at least partial reworking has occurred to the produce).

The role of Britain becoming a trade gateway to the EU is best served by remaining in the EEA. Membership of the EEA will also grant the UK the right to access the single market in services and procurement. With Britain's traditional strength in these sectors the UK can continue as a base for third-country subsidiaries to access the EU.

This will give countries around the globe a significant reason to enter into free trade agreements with the UK. EU trade agreements include the export of regulations which harm competitiveness. As such, the UK will be a preferable route for businesses to access the EU's internal market. If the UK can expand its free trade agreements beyond those the EU has made then businesses in the EU will also be able to benefit from using the UK as a location where value can be added to the production process.

This process will also make the UK a more effective link between North America and the Single Market. The Commonwealth and other overseas trade deals therefore augment EFTA/EEA membership and vice versa.

Conclusion

Given the political realities, there are a number of good reasons for the UK to leave the EU and rejoin EFTA and remain in the European Economic Area. However, its decisions may have wider ramifications and benefits. Firstly, there is no contradiction in both Britain's strategy for change in Europe and its approach to global trade via the Commonwealth. For the UK, trade with both EFTA and the Commonwealth was and still is compatible.

Other nations may follow Britain. For example, an opinion poll in Denmark found that more than twice as many of those asked would prefer EFTA membership to membership of the

EU.[33] Furthermore, if life outside the EU proves to be viable, then other threats to leave the union would need to be taken seriously and this could lead to a brake on further powers being handed to Brussels. An example of this process happened in Canada – among the most decentralised countries in the world largely because the state of Quebec has on occasion threatened to withdraw from the union.

Rejoining EFTA makes sense on both economic and political grounds. It allows the UK a formal role in EU/EEA discussions and is also likely to prove popular with the British public.[34] This is not surprising with EFTA member states enjoying lower unemployment and higher standards of living than their EU counterparts. In fact, polls have consistently shown members of the British public favouring a 'looser' relationship with the EU when offered such an option.

Britain can lead by example and show that there are alternatives available. The UK led in the formation of the European Free Trade Association in 1960 as an alternative to the European Economic Community, which was to become in time the European Union. If the UK can actively promote different options from EU membership, and make them a success, then other countries may wish to join the UK in a more successful alliance. Or at the very least threaten to do so.

The potential for decentralisation of the political union following a member state's exit is a very real one. According to the German academic, Professor Roland Vaubel, the exit of one state will encourage other states to seek a return of powers. This could recreate competition between member states as civil servants and politicians search for innovative ways to achieve a competitive advantage over their rivals. This could include reducing the level of both

33 YouGov Poll, 18 January 2012, found that 44 per cent of Danes are pro-EFTA while just 21 per cent want to remain in the EU.

34 http://www.brugesgroup.com/eu/71-said-they-would-prefer-britain-to -leave-the-eu-and-join-efta.htm?xp=comment

taxation and regulation – arguably the two main negative effects of the EU's system of government. The EU not only imposes high regulation but seeks to limit tax competition and sets minimum, not maximum, levels of taxation in areas such as value added tax and opposes levels of corporation tax that it deems too low. At the very least it will give EU citizens the opportunity to compare and contrast their neighbour's policies with those in their own country. Brexit can dramatically change the status quo in Europe and per-haps end the drift towards ever closer union.

Appendix A. The alternatives

	UK in EU	EFTA / EEA	Customs Union	EU bilateral	WTO
New regulations per year	1000+	350	Negotiation	200[a]	0
Financial contributions per year & per capita[b]	£15 billion £243 per capita	£6.5 billion £106 per capita[c]	£0	£3.25 billion £53 per capita	£0
Accounts approved by auditors	Never	Every year	N/A	N/A	N/A
Employees	30,000+	90	0	Committees	0
Input into EU law making	Yes	Yes	No	No	No
Control over fisheries	EU	UK	UK	UK	UK
Control over agriculture	EU	UK	UK	UK	UK
Involvement in home affairs	EU	UK	UK	UK	UK
Involvement in justice	EU	UK	UK	UK	UK
Free movement of goods	Yes	Yes	Yes	Yes	5.5% tariff[d]

[a] Swiss adopted 2,000 EU regulations: http://blogs.telegraph.co.uk/news/danielhannan/100186074/
[b] EEA/EFTA commitment and grants figures converted from EUR to GBP at 2011 annual average exchange rates (HM Treasury European Union Finances 2012; EFTA 51st Annual Report, 2011. And Leaving the EU, House of Commons Research Paper 13/42).
[c] This is if the UK continues to participate in EU programmes.
[d] http://stat.wto.org/TariffProfiles/E27_E.htm

	UK in EU	EFTA / EEA	Customs Union	EU bilateral	WTO
Free movement of services	Yes	Yes	No	No	No
Free movement of capital	Yes	Yes	No	Yes	No
Free movement of people	Yes	Can restrict	No	No	No
Mutual recognition	Yes	Yes	No	No	No
UK tax sovereignty	Partial[e]	Yes	Yes	Yes	Yes
Approximate number of EU laws	21,321[f]	4,179	Negotiation	2,000 est.	0
Two European Parliaments	Yes	No	No	No	No
European Arrest Warrant	Yes	No	No	No	No
Estimated annual economic cost	10% of GDP[g]	£7.5 bn[h]	N/A	Minimal	5.5% MFN
Office in Brussels	Yes	Yes	No	No	No
Website	Yes	Yes	No	No	Yes
Member of NATO	Yes	Yes	Yes	Yes	Yes
Common Foreign Policy	Yes	No	No	No	No
Tariff free imports	No	Yes	No	Yes	Yes
Ability to make bilateral free trade agreements	No	Yes	No	Yes	Yes
Active in WTO	No	Yes	No	Yes	Yes
Transparency	Treaties	Convention	Bilateral	Bilateral	N/A
Pages in legal document	200+	30	61	Complex	Complex
Prominent member	UK	Norway	Turkey	Switzerland	Russia
unemployment rate	7.1%	3.3%	8.8%	4%	5.4%
Time to switch from the EU	N/A	Weeks – current EEA member	Years – negotiate agreement	Years – negotiate agreement	Need to agree trade schedules

[e] EU control over indirect taxation, *Coordinating Member States' direct tax systems in the Internal Market*, ECOFIN.

[f] http://eur-lex.europa.eu/en/legis/latest/index.htm

[g] Congdon (2012: 16).

[h] The recurrent annual cost to UK businesses from EU-origin regulations. Source: British Chamber of Commerce, Burdens Barometer 2010. And, UK-EU economic relations – key statistics, House of Commons Library, SN/EP/6091, 13 February 2013, page 6.

Appendix B. Additional benefits of EFTA/EEA membership

Finance	
Access to the internal market without financial liability	Access to Single Market without the debt liability to the European Investment Bank (€35.7bn UK liability) and the ESFM where €6 billion liability still remains.
Financial savings	£180 per capita.
Economic management	
Control over fishing resources	Reclaiming UK waters will give the UK control over a resource worth £4.5bn per year.
Control over agriculture	Cheaper food. The OECD estimate that the CAP, its taxes and protectionism costs a family of four $1,000 per year.
Reduction in regulation	There will be a two thirds reduction in the rate of new regulations. If just two fifths of the EU inspired red tape can be disposed of then economic output will increase by 2 per cent.
Trade	
Develop own trade and investment links	Members of both EFTA and the European Economic Area are free to deliver their own trade agreements.
Investor resolution of disputes	Through the EEA institutions businesses can force the EU to comply with the terms of the EEA agreement.
Limit threat of EU anti-dumping action	EEA members are less likely to face anti-dumping action on exports to the EU. A liberal anti-dumping policy can reduce the price of imported consumables by £30bn. [a]
Mutual recognition of goods	Regulation EC 764/2008 demands that goods that are legally sold in one EEA country can be sold in another.
Easy access to services market	EEA members have full access to the EU's services market.
Access to public procurement	Continued access to a market that is worth €2,150bn per year which was in 2008 around 16% of EU GDP. [b]
Influence over EU law	
Policy shaping	Representatives of the EEA/EFTA states and their businesses are involved in 500 EU working groups.
Achievability	
Will the EU agree to continued UK membership of the EEA?	UK is already a member of the EEA. Norway and Switzerland have existing trade agreements with the EU dating from 1973. Britain does not have that advantage and will therefore need to rely on EEA membership.

[a] Minford et al. (2005).

[b] http://www.efta.int/eea/policy-areas/goods/competition-aid-procurement-ipr/procurement

Financial Services	
Measures that may harm the City of London do not apply	EU rules relating to financial services do not have EEA relevance and therefore do not apply to EFTA/EEA states.
Immigration	
Immigration can be restricted in the EEA	Liechtenstein, an EEA member, uses Article 112 and 113 and Protocol 15 of the EEA agreement to restrict immigration.

Appendix C. Problems with the Swiss option

Trade	
Investor dispute resolution	Exporters do not have a mechanism by which they can force the European Union to comply with the terms of the bilateral agreements.
Mutual recognition of produce	There is no mutual recognition of standards. Regulatory developments in the EU can create barriers preventing Swiss businesses from exporting unless the Swiss update their law and bring it into line with EU rules.
Easy access to the EU's services market	Businesses based in Switzerland do not have the right to take part in the services Single Market. The EU's FTAs often do not include services.
Transparency	
Decisions on what EU laws apply are made by numerous committees	The decision-making process by which Switzerland is obliged to adopt some EU standards and regulations has little transparency. Even the European Commission has objected to the overly bureaucratic nature of the bilateral trade agreements.
Influence over EU law	
There are few formal mechanisms by which the Swiss can influence EU law	Decisions on whether or not Switzerland adopts EU law are thought to rest on threats made by the EU that, unless there is compliance, the EU will cancel the bilateral trade agreements.
Achievability	
Will the EU agree to a Swiss style arrangement?	In the short and medium term it is unlikely that the EU will seek to replicate the Swiss model of relationships with the European Union.

References

Attwood, E. A. (1961) *The Agricultural Policies of Britain and Denmark*. London: Land. From Fram, N.: *Decolonization, the Commonwealth, and British Trade, 1945–2004*. Stanford University.

Bellis, R. (2003) Implementation of EU legislation. An independent study for the Foreign & Commonwealth Office.

Congdon, T. (2012) *How Much Does the European Union Cost Britain?* London: UK Independence Party.

Dustmann, C. and Frattini, T. (2013) The Fiscal Effects of Immigration to the UK. Discussion Paper Series CDP 22/13. Centre for Research and Analysis of Migration. http://www.cream-migration.org/publ_uploads/CDP_22_13.pdf

EFTA (2009) European Economic Area 1994–2009. European Free Trade Association. http://www.efta.int/media/publications/efta-commemorative-publications/eea15.pdf

EFTA (2013) EFTA in figures. *THIS IS EFTA 2013*. European Free Trade Association.

Ernst and Young (2013) Attractiveness survey UK 2013: No room for complacency. http://www.ey.com/Publication/vwLUAssets/Ernst-and-Youngs-attractiveness-survey-UK-2013-No-room-for-complacency/$FILE/EY_UK_Attractiveness_2013.pdf #page=37

Fernekeß, K., Palevičienė, S. and Thadikkaran, M. (2014) Trade and Investment Law Clinic Papers, *The Future of the United Kingdom in Europe: Exit Scenarios and Their Implications on Trade Relations*. Geneva, 7 January.

McNair, Lord (1961) *The Law of Treaties*, pp. 531–32; Leaving the EU, House of Commons Research Paper, 13/42.

Minford, P., Mahambare, V. and Nowell, E. (2005) *Should Britain Leave the EU: An Economic Analysis of a Troubled Relationship*. Cheltenham, UK: Edward Elgar.

North, R. (2013) *The Norway Option: Re-joining the EEA as an Alternative to Membership of the European Union*. London: The Bruges Group.

Pain, N. and Young, G. (2004) The macroeconomic impact of UK withdrawal from the EU. *Economic Modelling* 21(3) 387–408.

Stewart-Brown, R. and Bungay, F. (2012) *Rules of Origin in EU Free Trade Agreements*. Trade Policy Research Centre.

3 OLD LINKS, NEW TIES – GLOBAL FREE TRADE THROUGH THE ANGLOSPHERE AND COMMONWEALTH

Ralph Buckle and Tim Hewish

Introduction

The new global relationships for Britain lie in rejuvenated economic associations with Commonwealth nations and those with Anglosphere connections, such as the US, the Gulf States and Hong Kong. However, the goal should not be to swap one economic bloc for another. Instead, we argue that, in order for successful policy changes to take place, there must be a seismic shift in thought process away from large regional blocs to the concept of networks and soft power.

The Commonwealth is an underused network: English is its lingua franca and it can provide bilateral and multilateral trade and investment deals with a collection of like-minded nations. Despite this, Lord Howell was shocked during his time as Commonwealth Minister to find 'how little this is understood by many in this generation and circles who have been brought up to think that the Commonwealth is a relic of yesterday and that our destiny lies inside the European bloc' (Howell 2013: 46).

We do not argue for a Commonwealth-wide Free Trade Agreement (CFTA) due to its unrealistic, unwieldy and outdated nature. Neither is our approach one dimensional. Rather, the Commonwealth offers the chance for the UK to make favourable agreements with 52 other markets and also acts as a gateway to the rest of the world.

The considerable Commonwealth diaspora in the UK will also prove to be pivotal in building friendly business links. The last census found that 4.6 million people in the UK have a new Commonwealth background and many maintain ties.[1] The number from the old Commonwealth is harder to ascertain but it is clear why Lord Howell attested that 'Commonwealth blood is thicker than international water' (Howell 2013: 19).

However, no new policy will be effective unless it is accepted that we should move towards networked solutions not rigid blocs as a general policy aim. For decades, UK policy makers have understood the UK position through the lens of being a small European island off the Atlantic coast destined to be locked in with other European partners or as a Western power allied strongly to the US. This political bloc mentality of East vs West, Europe vs the rest, is a relic of 20th-century predicaments. The UK should not fit neatly into this outmoded space, but rather interlock loosely with various parts of a wider network.

Why the Commonwealth and Anglosphere nations?

Frankel (2000) identified the following factors as inhibitors to trade:

1. Lack of shared history/culture.
2. Lack of a free trade agreement (FTA).
3. Geographical factors.
4. Currency differences or volatilities.
5. Language differences.

In addition, we would add legal differences as a sixth factor.

---

1   2011 Census, The population of England and Wales, by ethnic group, BBC, 11 December 2012: http://www.bbc.co.uk/news/uk-20687168 (accessed 10 February 2014).

The UK has significant historical and cultural ties with Commonwealth and Anglosphere nations and the purpose of this section is to argue for more FTAs. However, we will also attempt to show that the other four potential barriers are significantly reduced or eliminated between Commonwealth and Anglosphere economies.

Geography

In the Internet age with an increasing percentage of Britain's trade being made up of services and digital goods, geographical factors are arguably becoming less relevant to trade patterns. As Lord Howell points out: 'Technology has trumped history and geography. In the digital age, size matters less and place matters less' (Howell 2013: 27).

Even so, history and geography can still have a major impact. For example, Frankel's analysis found that 'if two countries are not adjacent to each other, trade falls by half.' It is therefore fortunate that many of the potential geographic barriers do not stand in the way of trade with Commonwealth and Anglosphere economies.

The Commonwealth has immense geographical breadth. Almost all other economic and geopolitical blocs are based along regional lines. As a result they are particularly vulnerable to regional economic shocks, natural disasters, and political shifts. The Commonwealth, on the other hand, spans every inhabited time zone and continent making it the only true global network. In addition its members are also members of almost every other bloc, grouping and union, giving the UK the potential to gain proxy-access to almost every economy in the world by first focusing on its Commonwealth partners. Again, as Lord Howell explained: 'The modern Commonwealth... [offers] a golden gateway to the giant new markets beyond – China through Australia and still through Hong Kong from the inside, Brazil through Trinidad, and the Middle East' (Howell 2013: 55).

One of the other key geographical barriers to trade arises when a country is landlocked. An OECD Paper (2011) found that 'being landlocked reduces a typical country's openness ratio by 5 percentage points.' In addition, the Millennium Project Report (2005) found that the 'annual growth rate of landlocked developing countries [LLDCs] is 0.7% less than [for] coastal countries, as a consequence of their geographical location.' Even if firms are able to trade with landlocked nations, a UN office found that the costs of exporting to and importing from LLDCs are on average more than twice the costs of exporting to and importing from developing countries (UN-OHRLLS 2013).

This problem is not an issue for Commonwealth and Anglosphere countries as only seven of them do not have a coastline. Of these, all seven have at least one agreement in place with neighbouring Commonwealth countries to allow them access to ports. Furthermore, it is worth noting that after excluding island nations over 80 per cent of Commonwealth member states share a border with another.

Currency stability

With the Internet providing better information about currency fluctuations, freedom of capital movements leading to greater currency discipline in general and the confidence and security provided by payment systems such as PayPal, currency instability and the costs of exchange are arguably becoming less of a barrier to trade (Parcelforce 2013).

In general, the Commonwealth and Anglosphere still perform relatively well in relation to currency stability, though not as well as the EU. Sterling, the rand and the US, Canadian, New Zealand, Singapore and Australian dollars are all relatively stable currencies. In addition, a further 21 of Commonwealth or Anglo-sphere countries either use or are pegged to one of them. Firms that trade with a number of Commonwealth nations and territories may be able to do so while only monitoring one or two currencies. For example, a firm could trade with nine Commonwealth economies all by using the East Caribbean dollar, which is in turn pegged to the US dollar (as are five further Commonwealth currencies).

Language

Around 1.75 billion people speak English to a reasonable level (British Council 2013). Those who speak English as a first language are responsible for an estimated 28.2 per cent of global GDP.[2] In many countries the English language also acts as a stabilising factor bringing together disparate ethnic groups and tribes under a unified language in which they all have an equal footing. This has been particularly documented in Nigeria[3] and India.[4] Thus, as we trade and build links with other Anglosphere countries, we will not only reap the mutually beneficial rewards, but also help stabilise and unite our trading partners.

The most obvious impact of maximising trade with English-speaking nations is the reduced costs to businesses from not needing to pay for translators, language training for staff or pay higher wages to multilingual employees (or, alternatively, accept lower non-language skills). This can be particularly important for SMEs, many of whom are so called 'accidental exporters' who

---

2   Unicode Technical Note #13: GDP by Language: http://www.unicode.org/notes/tn13/tn13-1.html

3   Language as a tool for national integration: the case of English language in Nigeria: http://www.ijalel.org/viewpdf.aspx?articleid=131

4   English has helped unite the diverse 'cultures' of India: http://www.deccanherald.com/content/348329/english-has-helped-unite-diverse.html

post their goods or services online and suddenly find themselves with an international market.

There are also far more tangible benefits to focusing our initial efforts on English-speaking countries. Ghemawat showed that two countries that share a common language trade 42 per cent more with each other than two identical nations that lack the same bond. Pinker (1994) observed that 'a common language connects the members of a community into an information-sharing network with formidable collective powers.'

Integration will increase once trade barriers are reduced. An Economist Intelligence Unit (EIU 2012) study of executives at internationally facing businesses found that 64 per cent said differences in language and culture make it difficult to gain a foothold in unfamiliar markets. A British Council (2012) study also found that people from other countries speaking English resulted in a significant increase in 'the average level of trust in people in the UK,' which in turn contributed to a 'higher level of interest in doing business and trade with the UK.'

The opportunities of trade with English-speaking nations are also growing. The English-speaking population is estimated to reach 2 billion by the end of this decade (British Council 2013). The EF English Proficiency Index found an increasing trend in almost all target markets, including all the BRIC nations and key Asian economies.[5]

Moreover, a YouGov poll found that 68 per cent of Chinese citizens wished to learn the language[6] while *The Economist* found that 86 per cent of Chinese Executives polled expect that 50 per cent of their employees will need to know English if their companies are to make a success of their international plans (EIU 2012). In addition, a multitude of international companies including

---

5   EF EPI trends: http://www.ef.co.uk/epi/analysis/ef-epi-trends/

6   http://cdn.yougov.com/cumulus_uploads/document/rg1lebivab/YG-Archive -140121-ChinaData.pdf

Nokia, SAP, Heinkeken, Rakuten, Samsung, Renault and Lenovo are all adopting English as a single corporate language across their global operations.

It is also worth bearing in mind that much of what the UK services exports would expect above average benefits from more trade integration with English-speaking economies. Finance is the most obvious of these, with the top four financial centres in the world all speaking English along with a further ten in the top 25,[7] while English is widely acknowledged as the 'language of the markets' around the world.[8]

Another sector that would benefit is education and training, the export of which currently generates £17.5bn (BIS 2013). Obviously, not all of this is reliant on the English language, but much is and a significant portion involves teaching the language itself (around £2.3bn (BIS 2011)). In addition to this, UK universities are setting up campuses around the world.[9] The same argument applies to creative industries, which generate around £16bn in exports.[10] The creative industries would not only flourish with a renewed focus on English-speaking countries, their growth would also help spread knowledge of the language further.

Legal systems

The Commonwealth does not just speak English, it *thinks* English. This is most visible and relevant in respect of the common law. The common law is prevalent throughout Commonwealth

---

7   The Global Financial Centres Index 14: http://www.longfinance.net/images/ GFCI14_30Sept2013.pdf

8   Mishal Husein of BBC World: http://youtube/3zaTCI_65j4?t=30s

9   Global Higher Education: Branch campus listing: http://www.globalhighered.org/ branchcampuses.php

10 CBI: Creative industries in focus: http://www.cbi.org.uk/business-issues/ creative-industries/in-focus/

nations and the US.[11] Around 40 per cent of Commonwealth countries use common law and over 42 per cent have a mixed system.[12]

In addition, a common law system can have significant impact on encouraging current exporters to increase their overseas activity. An Institute of Directors' survey[13] found that 30 per cent of exporters identified 'overseas regulations/legislation' as a reason why they did not export more. While this will always be a factor in any foreign market, the relatively recognisable and familiar common law systems prevalent around the Commonwealth and Anglosphere would see this impact reduced.

This impact should not be underestimated. As Roumeen Islam and Ariell Reshef (2006) have found: 'Different legal origins do have a detrimental effect on trade, between 10% and 25%.'

Current economic trends

Growth and trade

The Commonwealth is catching up with and will overtake the EU with regard to their share of world national income. This is illustrated by Figure 5, which shows the national income shares for the Commonwealth and the euro zone and the original EEC that the UK joined in 1973 (the euro zone is shown on the left and the 1973 definition of the EEC on the right).

---

11 *Countries that Use Common Law,* The Encyclopaedia of New Zealand, http://www.teara.govt.nz/en/interactive/33931/countries-that-use-common-law (accessed 14 September 2013).

12 CIA World Factbook: Field listing: Legal system: https://www.cia.gov/library/publications/the-world-factbook/fields/2100.html (accessed 5 February 2014).

13 IoD: Ice Skates to Argentina: IoD Member Export Trends 2012–13: http://www.iod.com/influencing/policy-papers/enterprise-and-business-environment/iod-skates-to-argentina-iod-member-export-trends-201213 (accessed 10 September 2013).

Figure 5   Commonwealth and Europe share of real world GDP (PPP, $bn)
1970–2013

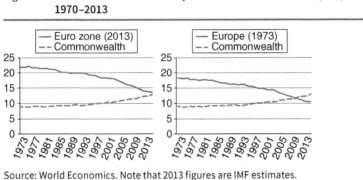

Source: World Economics. Note that 2013 figures are IMF estimates.

The gap in GDP between the euro zone and the Commonwealth has decreased so rapidly that they were almost level on
18% of the world's GDP in 2013, while the EEC of 1973 was over-
taken by the Commonwealth in 2009.[14] World Economics projects
that this trend will continue and accelerate in the next 20 years.

When it comes to trade, it is notable that UK exports to the EU
are predominantly to five countries, of which Ireland is one. Our
main trading relationships are with a small number of countries
rather than with the EU as a whole. At the same time, the UK
provides one sixth of all EU exports to Singapore, Australia and
India, one fifth of EU exports to Canada and almost one fifth of
EU exports to the US.[15] In other words, the UK already has extensive exports to Commonwealth and Anglosphere countries.

Business and corruption rankings

Many Commonwealth and Anglosphere countries that should
be a priority for an FTA are very good places with which to trade

14 http://www.worldeconomics.com/papers/Commonwealth_Growth
_Monitor_0e53b963-bce5-4ba1-9cab-333cedaab048.paper?PaperID=
0E53B963-BCE5-4BA1-9CAB-333CEDAAB048

15 Ibid, p. 75.

Table 14 **World Bank's Ease of Doing Business rankings**	
Rank	*Economy*
1	Singapore
2	Hong Kong
3	New Zealand
4	United States
5	Denmark

Source: http://www. doingbusiness .org/rankings

Table 15 **World Bank's 'Starting a Business' rankings**	
Rank	*Economy*
1	New Zealand
2	Canada
3	Singapore
4	Australia
5	Hong Kong

Source: http://www. doingbusiness .org/rankings

Table 16 **World Bank's 'protecting investors' rankings**	
Rank	*Economy*
1	New Zealand
2	Singapore
3	Hong Kong
4	Malaysia
5	Canada

Source: http://www. doingbusiness .org/rankings

and in which to do business. As Tables 14 – 16 show, the top places with which to do business, in which to start a business and which provide protection to investors are nearly all Commonwealth or Anglosphere countries. Table 17 suggests that some EU countries (mainly Scandinavian) are among the least corrupt but, even by this metric, Anglosphere and Commonwealth countries are well represented. Indeed, if only high-income countries are considered, Commonwealth and Anglosphere countries have a much higher average score when it comes to corruption than EU countries.

When it comes to economic freedom, five of the six nations identified as entirely economically free by the Heritage Foundation Index of Economic Freedom are Commonwealth or Anglosphere countries (the other being Switzerland).

When taken together, these incredibly strong statistics show convincingly that the UK can be confident in making trustworthy and healthy FTAs with a significant number of Commonwealth and Anglosphere partners which share our values, legal systems and potential for long-term prosperity. Box 6 provides some background for one country about its economy, legal system and so on, which demonstrates that it has a promising starting point for the development of fuller trading relationships if the protectionism of the EU can be jettisoned.

Table 17 **The Corruption Perception Index**

Rank	Country	Rank	Country
1	New Zealand	5	Norway
1	Denmark	7	Switzerland
3	Finland	8	Netherlands
3	Sweden	9	Australia
5	Singapore	9	Canada

Source: http://www.transparency.org/cpi2013/results

Small countries with the right approach can broker major FTAs. A liberated and global-facing UK should have little trouble doing the same with its far larger market and political influence.

The Internet

The Internet will undoubtedly prove to be one of the biggest drivers of trade and prosperity in the 21st century. This will be particularly important to the UK as a world leader in digital goods. *The Economist* recently described the British as the 'digital shop-keepers of the world' and pointed out the significant contribution the Internet makes to our economy.[16]

Once again, the Anglosphere has an advantage in this area. With almost 85 per cent of homepages and an estimated 55 per cent of all Internet content in English, it has never been easier for British SMEs to reach the world.[17]

This advantage could be key. The benefits to businesses are significant, especially to those businesses that export primarily through the Internet. The reduced need to provide multilingual versions of websites or translate adverts online can provide considerable time and cost savings.

Commonwealth markets represent significant important trading partners when it comes to business driven through the Internet. A number of them achieve Internet penetration well

16 Digital Shopkeepers of the World, *The Economist*: http://www.economist.com/blogs/graphicdetail/2012/04/daily-chart-2 (accessed 14 September 2013).

17 W3techs: Usage of content languages for websites: http://w3techs.com/technologies/overview/content_language/all (accessed 10 September 2013).

Box 6   New Zealand

New Zealand is an excellent example of what can be achieved when an economy takes a global approach and focuses on trade, an approach that resulted in it being the first developed economy to sign a free trade agreement with China in 2008.[1] It also already has trade agreements with the ten ASEAN nations (and stronger individual agreements with Singapore, Malaysia, Thailand and Brunei), Australia, Hong Kong and Chile. New Zealand also has ongoing negotiations with India, South Korea, Russia, Belarus and Kazakhstan and is considering an agreement with Japan.

New Zealand ranks as the least corrupt country on earth and third in terms of ease of doing business. It tops the rankings in sub-indices such as starting a business and protecting investors. It is one of only six nations ranked as economically free by the Heritage Foundation and is the fifth highest economy for enabling trade according to the World Economic Forum.

1   The *New York Times*: China and New Zealand sign free trade deal: http://www
.nytimes.com/2008/04/07/business/worldbusiness/07iht-7tradefw.11718461
.html?_r=0

above their geographical neighbours. In Africa, there are over 89m Commonwealth Internet users, representing 53 per cent of the continent's total users.[18] In South East Asia, despite the Commonwealth population only making up 5.6 per cent of the region's total, Commonwealth countries make up 13.5 per cent of its Internet users. While the regional average Internet penetration is only 31.6 per cent, the average figure in Commonwealth economies is 71.2 per cent.[19]

---

18   Calculated from Internet Usage Statistics: http://www.Internetworldstats.com/
stats1.htm (accessed 18 January 2014).

19   Ibid.

By developing free trade relationships with Commonwealth and Anglosphere countries, the UK can not only avoid or reduce many of the non-tangible trade barriers it might expect to face elsewhere, but also reap the significant advantages of existing trends and the ever-growing importance and power of the Internet, which will make geographical closeness much less important.

Should Britain join an enlarged NAFTA?

The first example we will consider for promoting free trade in the Anglosphere and Commonwealth is the possibility of expanding the North American Free Trade Agreement (NAFTA) to include the UK. Many commentators have cited this possibility. However, it is a policy plagued by outdated features. NAFTA is dated and does not address items such as finance, which are central to the UK–US economic dynamic. Furthermore, each NAFTA member would have the right to veto any arrangement with the UK. Mexico may do so given that its trade with the UK is low and that it has a preference for other Central American nations to join.

Instead, the US and the UK could craft a new free trade agreement which included investment and finance.

Britain is the largest foreign investor in the US. As of 2011, the UK had $442 billion invested, representing 17 per cent of the $2.5tn of foreign direct investment, while the US has 902,000 workers in jobs created and sustained by British companies (CBI 2012).

An issue that clouds a possible UK–US free trade agreement is the conclusion of the Transatlantic Trade and Investment Partnership (TTIP) deal between the US and EU, which could well have taken place by 2017. If that is indeed the case, then the UK would already have a free trade agreement with the US, via the EU. Because the Lisbon Treaty now explicitly allows member states to exit, the US could ask for some sort of mechanism which allows the free trade agreement to remain in place for exiting members of the EU. This would be open to legal challenges and the EU would certainly not allow a deal that was struck by the EU Trade Commission to be signed by the individual nations as it would undermine the whole principle of the European Union. However, if the TTIP is in operation by 2017, the US and UK could simply tweak the arrangements for mutual advantage and not go through the whole negotiating process from scratch. This would mean a deal could take months and not years to come into effect. This same would also be true for an agreement with Canada as the EU already has a free trade agreement with that country (CETA).

EFTA – a possible stopgap?

There have been debates about the UK's options in relation to EFTA, the EEA or the so-called Swiss model. We propose that the UK should sidestep this issue and, instead, obtain a free trade agreement with the EU, treating it as any other nation anywhere. However, this is not to say that seeking membership of EFTA is insignificant. In fact, it could be a vital and rapid tool for the UK to secure free trade agreements with third parties.

We view EFTA differently from many other commentators. We see EFTA as a gateway to join free trade agreements that EFTA already has so that the UK does not have to conduct its own separate deal with all of EFTAs current free trade agreement partners (which has taken them over 20 years to craft). By joining EFTA, the UK would inherit trade deals under Article 56 (3) of the EFTA Convention:

> Any State acceding to this Convention shall apply to become a party to the free trade agreements between the Member States on the one hand and third states, unions of states or international organisations on the other.[20]

---

20 EFTA Convention, Article 56 (3): http://www.efta.int/sites/default/files/ documents/legal-texts/efta-convention/Vaduz%20Convention%20Agreement.pdf (accessed 22 January 2014).

What is notable is the Commonwealth thread running through its agreements to date – Canada, the South African Customs Union, Singapore, Hong Kong and the Gulf States – while EFTA also is in advanced talks with India and Malaysia. Therefore, if the UK were to secure accession, it would be party to 24 free trade agreements covering 33 nations. As EFTA is not a customs union it also allows its countries to conduct free trade agreements with other parties. Therefore, the UK could try and strengthen these current deals as a group or go it alone and build upon what is already established.

Any nation looking to join EFTA is subject to veto from any member and the decision will be political rather than economic. A UK application to join may be subject to particular scrutiny given the UK's size economically, politically and in terms of population.

That said, the UK founded EFTA in 1960. The UK would be rejoining an organisation that it left: it even created the Convention itself. EFTA already appears on the UK statute book and it would be easier to reverse a law than forge one from scratch.[21] The UK abolished the Act when it joined the EEC in 1972.[22]

The UK return is touched upon by Schwok and Jayj. Their sources within EFTA explained that unlike the EU it does not pursue an active enlargement policy and that: 'Feasibility and desirability of a possible EFTA enlargement would have to be assessed on a case-by-case basis for each possible applicant.'[23] They go on to show that there is no guarantee that EFTA nations

---

21 Historic Hansard, HC Deb, 14 December 1959, vol. 615: http://hansard
.millbanksystems.com/commons/1959/dec/14/european-free-trade
-association#S5CV0615P0_19591214_HOC_343 (accessed 22 January 2014).

22 European Communities Act 1972, http://www.legislation.gov.uk/ukpga/1972/68/
schedule/3/part/I (accessed 22 January 2014).

23 UK returning to EFTA: Divorce at 40 and going back to Mom and Dad?, Point 78,
p. 10: http://www.publications.parliament.uk/pa/cm201213/cmselect/cmfaff/
writev/futunion/m21.pdf

would welcome new members and that the bloc itself its 'quite homogenous' in terms of size, economic development and trade preferences. Therefore, bigger nations such as the UK would, in their own analysis, 'shake the established base of the whole organisation'.[24]

Any potential agreement with EFTA could have opt-outs for the UK, which would mean that it would not be bound by the EFTA–EU trade agreement through the EEA. That way, the UK would not be impinging on EFTA's carefully crafted and close deal with the EU. This, of course, would be a fluid arrangement and subject to change during any application process. There is also a joining fee for EFTA membership, but this is very small compared with the costs of EU, EEA or the Swiss bilateral deals. Finally, the UK's power and economic influence has so far been seen as negative, but, on the other hand, an EFTA strengthened by Britain in the international FTA arena would bolster EFTA's negotiating abilities.

In conclusion, our policy would be to have the UK make agreements with EFTA, while developing its main EU free trade agreement. We place a high, but secondary, importance on EFTA membership.

A trade deal down under: Australia and New Zealand

Australia has been a leading light in free trade agreements, especially with Commonwealth and Anglosphere countries. It has deals with the US, New Zealand, Singapore, Malaysia and ASEAN (AANZFTA) and it is negotiating deals with the Gulf States and India.[25] In most cases New Zealand follows suit and, as shown by

---

24 Ibid, Point 79, p. 10.

25 Australia's Trade Agreements, Australian Government Department of Foreign Affairs and Trade: http://www.dfat.gov.au/fta/ (accessed 24 January 2014).

AANZFTA, both nations worked together with ASEAN to form the agreement.[26]

The first question is whether they would want to do a deal with an independent UK. In 2012 the then Australian Government drew up a whitepaper called *Australia in the Asian Century*, which could not have set out priorities more clearly (Australian Government 2012). However, under the current Abbott Government, reports have leaked that the white paper has been shelved.[27]

Abbott himself is a self-styled supporter of the Anglosphere and has made a number of comments regarding widening it to include its Asian branches: 'As with all the countries that think and argue among themselves in English (that these days include Singapore and Hong Kong, Malaysia and even India), what we have in common is usually more important than anything that divides us.'[28]

Once the reality of a British exit from the EU became apparent, it is likely that the expansionist trade policies of both Australia and New Zealand would make a trade deal feasible. Furthermore, Australia is the UK's 17th largest export market for goods and 7th for services. The UK is also an important market for Australia. The shared language and legal system should make a free trade agreement easy to achieve in principle. However, there must be the political will to do so on both sides. A newly separated but networked Commonwealth Office would help facilitate an agreement.

---

26 Trade Relations and Agreements, New Zealand Ministry of Foreign Affairs and Trade: http://www.mfat.govt.nz/Trade-and-Economic-Relations/2-Trade-Relationships-and-Agreements/index.php (accessed 24 January 2014).

27 Asian Century plans consigned to history, *The Australian*, 28 October 2013: http://www.theaustralian.com.au/national-affairs/policy/asian-century-plans-consigned-to-history/story-e6frg8yo-1226747866681# (accessed 25 January 2014).

28 Abbott, T., Address to Queen's College, University of Oxford, 14 December 2012: http://www.liberal.org.au/latest-news/2012/12/15/tony-abbott-transcript-address-queens-college-oxford-uk (accessed 25 January 2014).

The UK could try and forge separate deals with Australia and New Zealand, but these two nations are extremely close, as is highlighted by their joint FTA with ASEAN last year. Thus, it would make sense to try and either join ANZCERTA as a tripartite deal or create a new three-way FTA.

It is worth noting, however, that ANZCERTA is 31 years old so a deal may appear outdated for the UK, though joining ANZCERTA would be quicker and easier than starting from scratch.

A trade deal with ASEAN or its Commonwealth parts?

A newly independent UK has a number of Commonwealth partners in the Asia-Pacific region, other than Australia and New Zealand, that have been successfully building free trade agreements in the region and are internationally regarded as leading free-market economies. The two most notable are Malaysia and Singapore. They are also part of ASEAN, which has a strong record on free trade agreements. ASEAN also has a deal with India that covers goods, although India wants to extend this to services.[29]

We are not arguing that the UK joins ASEAN, as no Western nations have. Instead it should secure a bilateral deal with ASEAN much like Australia and New Zealand have done. This would allow the UK to tap into three Commonwealth markets as well as wider South East Asia in one go as opposed to developing separate bilateral agreements. This approach underscores our network approach to public policy which, when deployed through the Commonwealth, allows for greater purchase than working from a standing start. It also chimes with our goal of joining existing multilateral deals that have already spent years covering this ground.

---

29 Time we pushed ASEAN pact on services, Hindu Business line, 29 January 2014: http://www.thehindubusinessline.com/opinion/time-we-pushed-asean-pact-on-services/article5631395.ece (accessed 29 January 2014).

Moreover, another similar organisation that incorporates much of ASEAN is APEC – the Asia Pacific Economic Corporation. This association includes Western powers such as the US and Canada. It also has a long list of Commonwealth nations wishing to join, which are not along the Pacific Rim. Importantly, unlike the EU, APEC only exists to forward trading relations.[30]

Despite APEC not expanding since 1998 and freezing its membership, the UK should still make a formal approach as soon as possible. A 20-year pause is long enough given the significant economic upheavals between now and then. There are those in the organisation who fear that if India were to join, then it would tip the balance back in favour of Asia. However, we would argue that by allowing the UK and India to join this fear would be offset given the size of both economies.

Also, given the fact that it is not an FTA but an economic association, the feasibility of joining would not be slowed down by the minutiae of tariffs and quotas. Our Commonwealth partners should also be lobbied on the inside to assist the UK in its diplomatic efforts. That, after all, is the whole point of using the Commonwealth network – to be in multiple places at the same time across the world.

India – a remaining jewel

Without question India still represents the jewel in the crown for any nation looking to secure a trade deal, but this is by no means easy. India as a major rising power has been protectionist in its trade policy. India has very high agricultural tariffs averaging between maximum bound rates of 100 per cent and 300 per cent.[31]

---

30 About APEC, Achievements and Benefits: http://www.apec.org/About-Us/About-APEC/Achievements-and-Benefits/Bogor-Goals.aspx (accessed 29 January 2014).

31 India adopting protectionist measures in agri, dairy sector, *India Times*, 14 March 2013: http://articles.economictimes.indiatimes.com/2013-03-14/

Additionally, intellectual property issues are unresolved, as pharmaceutical giant Pfizer has shown: 'India has systematically failed to interpret and apply its intellectual property laws in a manner consistent with recognized global standards.'[32]

To paint a bleaker picture, Vodafone was hit with a retrospective taxation charge a few years ago. This sent a clear signal that India was not fully open to the idea of foreign businesses.[33] Fortunately, the case was overturned by India's Supreme Court, which is largely free from corruption, and seen to fairly represent the rule of law. The *Wall Street Journal* commented: 'The tax case became a symbol for many foreign investors of the uncertainty of doing business in India, the unpredictability of regulators and the risks foreign firms face if they decide to make big bets on Indian growth.'[34]

Yet despite this uncertain environment the allure of India and the cultural leverage that the UK holds with India could prove useful. The UK is home to one of the largest populations from Indian descent outside mainland India with 1.4 million; only the US, out of a population of 300 million, has more, with 1.9 million.[35]

news/37713839_1_cent-tariff-protectionist-measures-export (accessed 29 January 2014).

32 US business bemoans India trade 'protectionism', Yahoo News, 13 March 2013: http://news.yahoo.com/us-business-bemoans-india-trade-protectionism -183556984--finance.html (accessed 29 January 2014).

33 Vodafone steps up tax row with India, BBC, 17 April 2012: http://www.bbc.co.uk/ news/business-17746649 (accessed 29 January 2014).

34 Vodafone overturns tax bill in India, *Wall Street Journal*, 21 Jan 2013: http:// online.wsj.com/news/articles/SB10001424052970204616504577172152700710334 (accessed 29 January 2014).

35 Indians are third largest immigrant group in US, *Times of India*, 23 August 2013: http://articles.timesofindia.indiatimes.com/2013-08-23/us-canada-news/ 41440115_1_11-percent-migration-policy-institute-5-percent (accessed 29 January 2014).

As mentioned previously the English language will play a significant role in the development of relationships with India. An English-language newspaper in India set out this most succinctly:

> Modern India's unique selling proposition to attract FDI is obviously what can be called, 'the English speaking dividend' that has aided the economic growth. English is not a foreign language anymore in India ... Today English is perceived as a language, which helps its diverse population to communicate in a country endowed with over 6,500 languages/dialects ... English is symbolic of the language of opportunity.[36]

In terms of Commonwealth free trade agreements with India, the potential is even greater. Currently, New Zealand, Australia and Canada are developing free trade agreements with India. Australia's joint study found that a completed free trade agreement would increase both countries' national income by more than 1 per cent. Canada has predicted that its GDP would grow by $15bn and India's by $6bn with a free trade agreement.[37] South Africa is also pushing for an Indian preferential trade pact in relation to goods[38] and other Commonwealth partners have a goods trade deal with India through ASEAN.

If this wide range of Commonwealth nations is trying to strike deals with India, then this leaves the potential for the UK to do likewise. However, the deals are slow and subject to dogged

---

36 English has helped unite the diverse 'cultures' of India, *Deccan Herald*, 31 July 2013: http://www.deccanherald.com/content/348329/english-has-helped-unite -diverse.html (accessed 29 January 2014).

37 Canada-India Free Trade Agreement Negotiations, Foreign Affairs, Trade and Development Canada: http://www.international.gc.ca/trade-agreements -accords-commerciaux/agr-acc/india-inde/info.aspx?lang=eng (accessed 1 February 2014).

38 Talks on for preferential trade pact between India, South Africa, *Times of India*, 4 September 2013: http://articles.economictimes.indiatimes.com/2013-09-04/ news/41765859_1_preferential-trade-pact-south-africa-bilateral-trade (accessed 1 February 2014).

negotiations from a still somewhat protectionist India. The proposed Commonwealth Office should see this possible free trade agreement as one of the biggest prizes for its department, but it should expect a protracted deal.

South Africa – the gateway to Commonwealth Africa?

South Africa is often seen a leading nation in Africa. It describes itself as the gateway to Africa. It is the highest-ranked African economy in the world. However, this is being challenged as other parts of Africa, notably Commonwealth, become more stable. *The Economist* pointed out that:

> The economy of Nigeria, with some 158m people to South Africa's 50m, has been roaring along at an annual rate of almost 7% for the past eight years—and may even become Africa's biggest by 2016 ... At the same time, Ghana and Kenya are competing with South Africa to host the African headquarters of foreign multinationals.[39]

Although, the magazine caveats these trends by adding:

> Yet South Africa's decline is only relative. Despite having the continent's fifth-biggest population, it still has easily its biggest economy, with GDP per head of over $11,000 PPP, bigger than China's or India's and more than four times the African average. Its infrastructure is by far the best in Africa. It has 80% of the continent's rail network and is home to the region's biggest stock exchange. It also has the biggest middle class, proportional to its population, of any African country.[40]

39 The gateway to Africa?, South Africa's business pre-eminence is being challenged, *The Economist*, 2 June 2012: http://www.economist.com/node/21556300 (accessed 1 February 2014).

40 Ibid.

The UK's relationship with South Africa is on paper quite strong. It claims that it sees South Africa as being in its *Premier League of trade partners*.[41] UKTI also indirectly acknowledges the Commonwealth factor in doing business in South Africa:

> Much of South Africa's legal, economic and business practices and legislation is based on the UK equivalents. This makes operating in South Africa less problematic and alien than in other international markets ... the cultural and historical links are broadly positive in the UK's favour. In return, the UK receives 4 out of every 5 South African investment projects in Europe.[42]

In terms of trading priorities within South African policy, the focus is almost wholly on intra-African unity. South Africa is part of the SACU customs union. The major example of a free trade agreement within African regions is the SADC-EAC-COMESA free trade agreement that will encompass 26 nations. It is this monumental deal and a free trade agreement with India, which are South Africa's current ongoing deals.[43]

Determining the prospects for a UK–South Africa trade agreement is difficult. However, as mentioned previously, if the UK were to secure EFTA membership it would enter into an EFTA-SACU deal that allowed for tariff reductions on goods. It would be easier for the UK to then build on this agreement within EFTA, perhaps to include services, rather than starting afresh. The UK would have the bargaining chip of not being subject to EU tariffs or quotas, which many African nations dislike. Thus a

---

41 UKTI – South Africa: http://www.ukti.gov.uk/export/countries/africa/ southernafrica/southafrica.html (accessed 1 February 2014).

42 Port Sector in South Africa, UKTI, 31 January 2014: http://www.ukti.gov.uk/ uktihome/item/705640.html (accessed 1 February 2014).

43 Trade Agreements, South Africa, Department of Trade and Industry: http://www .dti.gov.za/trade_investment/ited_trade_agreement.jsp (accessed 1 February 2014).

free trade policy throughout these discussions would prove to be a valuable tool.

This opens up the question of wider trade with Anglophone African countries which are growing rapidly. These nations still have close ties to the UK and share a language, laws and customs, but the UK fails to underscore this inbuilt mutual advantage. The only MP to point this out really is Shadow BIS Secretary, Chuka Umunna:

> The response from the Nigerian and Ghanaian business community is: 'Where are the Brits? Where have you been? You are historically, and still are, our preferred partner. You are reliable, you produce a quality product, we like your legal system and you deliver on time. But where have you been at the time when all have been coming to invest here? The British brand abroad is much stronger than we realise.[44]

His point is a valid one. The UK, in 2011, launched a new initiative called the African Free Trade initiative (AFTi), although its progress has not been reported back to parliament in any meaningful way since then.[45]

Drafting bilateral deals is much easier and quicker than drafting a multilateral deal. Separate deals with South Africa, Nigeria, Kenya and Ghana do not represent insurmountable challenges with a new Commonwealth Office working exclusively on Commonwealth trade deals.

Additionally, bilateral investment agreements should be used as an instrument to boost the prospect of free trade agreements

---

44 UK business must not miss out on Africa, This is Africa, 23 May 2013, http://www.thisisafricaonline.com/Business/UK-business-must-not-miss-out-on-Africa-Chuka-Umunna?ct=true (accessed 4 February 2014).

45 UK Government ramps up trading in Africa, 9 February 2011: https://www.gov.uk/government/news/uk-government-ramps-up-trading-in-africa (accessed 4 February 2014).

with these African nations and beyond. This competence was given to the EU in 2009.[46] Post-Brexit the UK would regain that ability, strengthening our hand in negotiations with Anglophone African nations that require such investment.

Moreover, the Anglophone nature of much trade should not be overlooked as has been already explained; but it remains paramount in Africa specifically. A British Council study (Coleman 2011) found that English was the preeminent language which united Africans in business on the continent.

The Gulf States

Although not Commonwealth nations, nor for that matter immediately identifiable as part of the Anglosphere, it can be argued that the Gulf States should form some part of our trade opportunities, which can be seen through a Commonwealth lens. To substantiate this claim we must touch upon the historical links. Bahrain, Kuwait, Qatar and the United Arab Emirates all became British protectorates during the 19th and early 20th centuries. They remained foreign territory, but their status placed them informally within the British Empire. This continued until Britain granted independence to Kuwait in 1961 and the remaining Gulf States in 1971 (Onley 2005). Strong ties still remain and this led the Foreign Affairs Select Committee to explain that:

> The Gulf had mattered to the UK for generations, and FCO described the UK's relationships in the Gulf as 'among our most enduring in the world' ... The fact that the Gulf wasn't directly colonised was generally thought to have resulted in a more

---

46 A letter from Mark Simmonds MP to Andrew Rosindell MP, 20 December 2012, In response to a Westminster Hall debate on Commonwealth Trade.

mutually respectful relationship and the UK now has a valuable legacy of close ties with a number of Gulf rulers.[47]

In a further demonstration of closer unity with the Gulf, the UK has been described as the Eighth Emirate after the UK's recent push to make it easier for people from Gulf States to visit through visa-free travel.[48] This accord is augmented through the proliferation of English in the Gulf, which is considered the primary second language, though competing with Arabic. It should also be noted that Bahrain and Kuwait use an English Common Law system.

In addition, the Royal United Services Institute released a report which comments that:

> There is some important ground to make up and the Gulf powers, in their military weakness and economic strength, are more pivotal to UK security and prosperity than was the case a decade ago. [For example,] Trade between the UK and the UAE reached £14 billion last year and the UAE alone invested £8 billion in UK projects. The biggest single group of UK expatriates – over 100,000 – live and work in the UAE. Qatar is believed to invest around £20 billion in the UK and may soon add another £10–15 billion in infrastructure investment. Qatar is, in any case, the prime supplier of liquefied natural gas (LNG) into the UK.[49]

---

47 The UK's relations with Saudi Arabia and Bahrain – Foreign Affairs Committee, Broader context: UK ties with the Gulf: http://www.publications.parliament.uk/pa/cm201314/cmselect/cmfaff/88/8806.htm (accessed 4 February 2014).

48 UK gives visa free travel to the Eighth Emirate to Emirates, *The National*, 12 November 2013: http://www.thenational.ae/uae/tourism/uk-gives-visa-free-travel-to-the-eighth-emirate-to-emiratis (accessed 4 February 2014).

49 A Return to East of Suez? UK Military Deployment to the Gulf, RUSI, 2012: http://www.rusi.org/publications/other/ref:N517AA8D59D1B3/

They conclude that there are 'compelling reasons for the UK to take its Gulf relationships much more seriously.'[50]

Post-Brexit, securing a free trade agreement and bilateral investment deal with the Gulf Cooperation Council (GCC), which also includes Saudi Arabia, is critical. In terms of bilateral trade with the region, the Gulf States are the UK's seventh largest export market.[51]

The UK is also developing potential in the Islamic finance sector.[52] This has an advantage with the wider Commonwealth, as a number of pivotal nations are Muslim and with which the UK can trade financial services. Last year the first World Islamic Economic Forum held in Europe took place in London.[53]

How does this leave the prospects for a free trade agreement in the Gulf? The GCC has a number of free trade agreements, one of which is with EFTA, but this has yet to come into force;[54] another is with Singapore.[55] The GCC is negotiating a deal with Australia[56] and the potential for deals with China[57] and India[58]

---

50 Ibid., p. 1.

51 Ibid.

52 Britain to become first non-Muslim country to launch sharia bond, *Daily Telegraph*, 29 October 2013: http://www.telegraph.co.uk/finance/newsbysector/banksandfinance/10410467/Britain-to-become-first-non-Muslim-country-to-launch-sharia-bond.html (accessed 4 February 2014).

53 9th WIEF, London http://wief.org/current-wief/ (accessed 4 February 2014).

54 EFTA Trade Agreements, GCC: http://www.efta.int/free-trade/free-trade-agreements/gcc (accessed 5 February 2014).

55 Overview of the GCC, The Singapore FTA Network, http://www.fta.gov.sg/fta_gsfta.asp?hl=32 (accessed 5 February 2014).

56 The Australian-GCC FTA agreement, Australian Government Department of Foreign Affairs and Trade: http://www.dfat.gov.au/fta/agccfta/ (accessed 5 February 2014).

57 GCC, China to sign "14-17 action plan, resume FTA negotiations, Bilaterals. org, 16 January 2014: http://www.bilaterals.org/?gcc-china-to-sign-14-17-action (accessed 5 February 2014).

58 Support early conclusion of FTA with GCC: India to Kuwait, Times of India, 8 November 2013: http://articles.economictimes.indiatimes.com/2013-11-08/

has also been revived. Interestingly, the EU tried to forge a deal with the Gulf as far back as 1988, but talks broke down and the GCC suspended them citing numerous unresolved issues.[59]

With the UK's strong historical and new trading relationship with the Gulf, we would argue that it is highly likely that both bilateral investment deals and a regional deal could be secured. Again EFTA accession would provide a ready-made option to build upon, although the UK independently would be in a good position to build agreements with the Gulf.

Hong Kong and China

We include consideration of Hong Kong and China because Hong Kong has a special place unofficially within the Commonwealth while China has used various Commonwealth organisations in order to promote trade. China sent 60 delegates to the 2011 Commonwealth Business Forum in Perth and repeated this in 2013 at Colombo with over 100 government and business leaders.[60] Furthermore, before Perth, Australia used Hong Kong as a staging post to invite Chinese business to understand the Commonwealth.[61] China uses Hong Kong's special relationship with a key number of Commonwealth nations to further its objectives. There is nothing stopping the UK from reverse engineering the

news/43822238_1_india-and-gcc-early-conclusion-economic-cooperation (accessed 5 February 2014).

59 GCC Members Suspend Free-Trade Talks With Europe, Bilaterals.org, 26 May 2010: http://www.bilaterals.org/?gcc-members-suspend-free-trade (accessed 5 February 2014).

60 Sri Lanka hopes for investment rise at record Commonwealth business meeting, Xinhuanet, 13 November 2013: http://news.xinhuanet.com/english/world/2013-11/13/c_132885572.htm (accessed 5 February 2014).

61 Australia's Commonwealth Business Forum launched in Hong Kong, Australian Consulate-General, Hong Kong, China, 28 April 2011: http://www.china.embassy.gov.au/hkng/PR_20110428.html (accessed 5 February 2014).

relationship with China – using the Commonwealth and Hong Kong to develop trade relationships with China.

This is underscored by the Director-General of the Hong Kong Economic and Trade Office, who revealed that British companies employed about 10 per cent of Hong Kong's workforce and that membership of the British Chamber of Commerce in Hong Kong is higher than anywhere else in Asia. She also made the point that the UK can make use of Hong Kong's geographical and economic position to enter emerging markets in Asia. Even more crucially she explains that the Closer Economic Partnership Arrangement (CEPA) between Hong Kong and China is in effect a free trade agreement which: 'UK companies can take advantage of because the beauty of CEPA is that it is nationality-blind: by setting up an operation in Hong Kong, foreign enterprises can use the city as their platform to enter the vast Chinese market.'[62] Moreover, UKTI highlights on its website that Hong Kong is the second largest market in Asia Pacific for UK goods exports and more than half of all the UK's investment in Asia is in Hong Kong.[63]

Hong Kong still has representation in numerous Commonwealth organisations; however, China does not grant associate or full membership. Andrew Rosindell MP made this point last year.[64] The question was side-stepped by the Chinese, but the point remains that, if China wishes to engage with the Commonwealth, then Britain should use its leverage in Hong Kong for the

---

62 Allcock, A., Director-General of the Hong Kong Economic and Trade Office, Why does Hong Kong still matter to the UK? Keynote at the Hong Kong Association, March 2011: http://international.lawsociety.org.uk/files/20101214_why_does_Hong_Kong_still_matter_to_the_UK.pdf

63 Building Britain's prosperity in Hong Kong, 21 March 2013: https://www.gov.uk/government/priority/building-britain-s-prosperity-in-hong-kong (accessed 5 February 2014).

64 British lawmaker to Beijing: Allow Hong Kong to rejoin Commonwealth, 11 November 2013: http://www.scmp.com/news/hong-kong/article/1352736/british-lawmaker-wants-hong-kong-back-commonwealth?page=all (accessed 5 February 2014).

mutual benefit of all three nations. In addition, Hong Kong uses a common law legal system.

The UK is also developing as the Western hub for offshore trading in the Chinese currency – the renminbi as well as the Western centre for Chinese investment.[65] Furthermore, it was agreed that the renminbi could be traded directly against sterling, rather than through the US dollar.[66]

Therefore, turning to free trade and the possibility of any deal, China is slowly opening up with the launch of its first Free Trade Zones.[67] Hong Kong also has a free trade agreement with EFTA which is far ahead of the EU's attempt at a deal. Therefore, any successful EFTA membership bid would grant the UK free access to the Hong Kong market.[68] The EFTA deal itself only took just over a year to be completed. Such speed and scope shows what can be achieved.

We would suggest that a trade agreement with Hong Kong could be concluded quickly and would be quite feasible. China would be somewhat more difficult, but it does have free trade agreements with a number of Commonwealth nations as well as with ASEAN, EFTA and Switzerland. It is also negotiating deals with the Gulf Council and Australia.[69] Nevertheless, achieving a free trade agreement with China would be slower than with Hong Kong.

---

65 The UK as the global centre for investment in China, HM Treasury infographic: http://www.flickr.com/photos/hmtreasury/10286451284/lightbox/ (accessed 5 February 2014).

66 Traders welcome latest UK-China deal on RMB, FX Week: http://www.fxweek .com/fx-week/news/2301379/traders-welcome-latest-uk-china-deal-on-rmb (accessed 5 February 2014).

67 Shanghai free trade zone attracts 1,400 companies, *Financial Times*: http://www. ft.com/cms/s/0/20b7714c-57fb-11e3-82fc-00144feabdc0.html#axzz2sXnxMLh2 (accessed 5 February 2014).

68 EFTA-Hong Kong FTA signed, EFTA, 21 June 2011: http://www.efta.int/about-efta/ news/2011-06-21-efta-hong-kong-fta-signed (accessed 5 February 2014).

69 China FTA Network, http://fta.mofcom.gov.cn/english/index.shtml (accessed 5 February 2014).

Summary

The UK will be extremely stretched in its capacity to create free trade agreements or bilateral investment agreements with all potential countries. The process will also require patience as the average free trade agreement takes around four years to complete. A deal with the US should be sought quickly and should run parallel to any EU free trade agreement. Indeed, the US tends to complete free trade agreements quickly, averaging 1.7 years Ferrantino (2006: 26). We expect the EU deal to be fraught, but not insurmountable as the EU is bound by the Lisbon Treaty to find an amicable solution.

EFTA creates complications as it could damage any EU deal. However, it does provide an important gateway to many other existing free trade agreements that would save the UK considerable time. EFTA deals with South Africa, Canada, the Gulf, Hong Kong, and hopefully India by 2017 will allow the UK more time to focus on other Commonwealth nations. We recommend that it is an approach worth pursuing.

Deals with Canada, Australia, New Zealand, Malaysia, Singapore and Hong Kong can probably be concluded relatively quickly – probably by 2021. A second phase of free trade agreements is likely to include nations such as South Africa, China, India, Nigeria, Ghana, Kenya or groups like ASEAN and this could be completed by 2023.

Conclusion

We have presented what we believe to be a visionary set of proposals that are reinforced by real world illustrations. These are not fanciful, but rather analytical projections of where the UK's destiny lies by way of a policy framework through a Commonwealth and Anglosphere perspective. This provides the political and relational context for the development of Britain as a global trading nation.

The Commonwealth's power lies in its networked approach thereby allowing the UK access to every continent and every time-zone as a collection of developed, developing and emerging economies. Its shared language of 1.75 billion English speakers facilitates trade and business ties, bringing greater stability and unity.

Furthermore, the fact that 2.55 billion citizens use a broadly common law legal system adds trust and safety to the Commonwealth system, as does its impressive business and corruption rankings. The Commonwealth is also the perfect decentralised entity from which the UK can import cheaper food and goods without EU tariffs. The UK has an inbuilt advantage of being the 'digital shop-keepers of the world'[70] as well as having numerous 'accidental exporters' backed by the language of international commerce and the Internet itself.

The British Government will need unlimited courage to complete the tasks set before them by Brexit. This chapter sets down a marker and a guide that will help ensure that the UK can trade freely as a global nation and is prosperous. Britain can, at once, be European, Atlantic and global whilst anchored within a Commonwealth context.

References

Australian Government (2012) *Australia in the Asian Century White Paper.* http://pandora.nla.gov.au/pan/133850/20130914-0122/asian century.dpmc.gov.au/white-paper.html (accessed 24 January 2014).

---

70 Digital Shopkeepers of the World, *The Economist*: http://www.economist.com/ blogs/graphicdetail/2012/04/daily-chart-2 (accessed 14 February 2014).

BIS (2011) *Estimating the Value to the UK of Education Exports.* http:// www.bis.gov.uk/assets/biscore/higher-education/docs/e/11-980 -estimating-value-of-education-exports.pdf

BIS (2013) *International Education: Global Growth and Prosperity.* https://www.gov.uk/government/uploads/system/uploads/attach ment_data/file/229844/bis-13-1081-international-education-global -growth-and-prosperity.pdf

British Council (2012) *Trust Pays: How International Cultural Relationships Build Trust in the UK and Underpin the Success of the UK Economy.* http://www.britishcouncil.org/sites/britishcouncil.uk2/files/trust -pays-report.pdf

British Council (2013) *The English Effect: The Impact of English, What It's Worth to the UK and Why It Matters to the World.* http://www. britishcouncil.org/sites/britishcouncil.uk2/files/english-effect -report.pdf

CBI 2012 *Sterling Assets IV: British Investment Creating U.S. Jobs*, p. 4. http://www.cbi.org.uk/media/1727518/sterling_assets_iv.pdf

Coleman, H. (2011) *Dream and Realities – Developing Countries and the English Language.* http://www.teachingenglish.org.uk/sites/teach eng/files/Z413%20EDB%20Section08.pdf (accessed 4 February 2014).

EIU (2012) *Competing Across Borders: How Cultural and Communication Barriers Affect Business.* Economist Intelligence Unit. www .economistinsights.com/sites/default/files/downloads/Competing %20across%20borders.pdf

Ferrantino, M. (2006) Policy anchors: do free trade agreements and WTO accessions serve as vehicles for developing-country policy reform?, Office of Economics Working Paper, US International Trade Commission. http://www.usitc.gov/publications/332/working_papers/EC20 0604A.pdf (accessed 10 February 2014).

Frankel, J. A. (2000) Assessing the efficiency gains from further liberalization. John F. Kennedy School of Government, Harvard University, Faculty Research Working Papers Series, RWP01-030.

Howell, D. (2013) *Old Links and New Ties: Power and Persuasion in an Age of Networks.* London: I. B. Tauris.

Islam, R. and Reshef, A. (2006) Trade and harmonization: if your institutions are good, does it matter if they are different? http://www-wds.worldbank.org/servlet/WDSContentServer/WDSP/IB/2006/05/02/000016406_20060502124637/Rendered/PDF/wps3907.pdf (accessed 5 February 2014).

Millennium Project (2005) *Millennium Project Report to the Secretary General.* http://www.unmillenniumproject.org/documents/MainReportComplete-lowres.pdf (accessed 8 February 2014).

OECD (2011) OECD Trade Policy Paper No. 116: Estimating the constraints to trade of developing countries http://www.oecd-ilibrary.org/trade/estimating-the-constraints-to-trade-of-developing-countries_5kg9mq8mx9tc-en (accessed 8 February 2014).

Onley, J. (2005) *Britain's Informal Empire in the Gulf, 1820–1971.* http://socialsciences.exeter.ac.uk/iais/downloads/Britain_s_Informal_Empire_in_the_Gulf_1820-1971_2005.pdf (accessed 4 February 2014).

Parcelforce (2013) *Overcoming Barriers to Export: A Guide for Growing Businesses by Parcelforce Worldwide and UK Trade & Investment.* http://www.parcelforce.com/sites/default/files/Exporters.pdf (accessed 10 September 2013).

Pinker, S. (1994) *The Language Instinct: The New Science of Language and Mind.* London: Penguin.

UN-OHRLLS (2013) *The Development Economics of Landlockedness: Understanding the Development Costs of Being Landlocked.* http://unohrlls.org/custom-content/uploads/2013/10/Dev-Costs-of-landlockedness.pdf (accessed 8 February 2014).

4   REVIVING THE AGE OF DRAKE: HOW A GLOBAL FREE-TRADE ALLIANCE (GFTA) CAN TRANSFORM THE UK

John C. Hulsman

'Disturb us, Lord, when we are too well pleased with ourselves,
When our dreams have come true because we have dreamed too little,
When we arrive safely because we sailed too close to the shore.'
'Disturb us, Lord, to dare more boldly, to venture on wider seas, where storms
Will show your mastery, where losing sight of land, we shall find the stars.'

> Excerpts from Drake's prayer, 1577, written in Portsmouth as
> he began his circumnavigation of the globe

Introduction: the benefits of thinking big

The basic intellectual problem with the endless, enervating, Jesuitical arguments surrounding the UK's place in Europe is that the debate has been far too myopic. It has concentrated on the minutiae of what concessions Prime Minister Cameron might just be able to pry from the clenched fists of his European partners, and how he would then transform this thin gruel into a convincing argument to sell to his sceptical public. In other words, it has been all about tactics, with precious little thought devoted to strategy, let alone the UK's dreams for the new era we find ourselves in.

This strikes me as exactly the wrong way to look at the question: it must be dreams and strategy first, tactics later. In other words, it's time UK policymakers rediscover the shrewd swashbuckling quality of Sir Francis Drake, who's almost unimaginably bold prayer opens my argument. For it must be remembered Drake wrote this paean to thinking big before he became the first captain to sail with his crew around the world (Magellan died along the way).

He was a visionary first – daring more boldly, losing sight of land and thus finding the stars – then fitted out his ship the Golden Hind to endure the privations ahead, and only then thought of the tactical navigation necessary to realise his dreams of glory. If the UK is to thrive in this new, dangerous, fascinating and far more rewarding era of globalisation, such an unorthodox manner of proceeding is absolutely necessary.

But such grandiose dreams and such bombastic thoughts simply do not jibe with today's zeitgeist. Here the British intellectual community is all about small ball, improving things at the margins, all the while remaining gloomily resigned to the fact that the UK is and will remain a power in relative decline. Echoing Drake, I'd say that such thinking becomes a self-fulfilling prophecy, dooming the UK to increasing irrelevance, as long as the country continues to sail 'too close to the shore.'

But there is an alternative to the commentariat's present gentle acquiescence in decline and failure. It lies in remembering the intellectual boldness of Drake and the other Elizabethans in changing the terms of the strategic game they were playing, in order to seize new advantages regarding heretofore entirely unthought-of opportunities. Oddly enough, in doing so the Elizabethans' insatiable global drive to open up inviting markets and facilitating trade beyond everything else is precisely the remedy again called for.

I propose that – following a 'no' vote in the referendum – the UK should change the very terms of the world it is living in, embracing and forming a Global Free Trade Alliance (GFTA), which will serve as the primary strategic policy for making the country fit for purpose in the challenging and exciting emerging age of globalisation.

Following such a repudiation of the EU, Her Majesty's Government will trigger Article 50 of the Lisbon Treaty, beginning the process of leaving the Brussels machinery. In the immediate aftermath – say over the following two years – the UK needs to focus intently on domestic measures to ready itself for the coming challenge of sailing into the unknown, while at the same time working out reasonable parting terms with its European neighbours.

Domestically, the government must pursue a policy of economic liberalism at home and free trade abroad. This interim period is more than ample time for the GFTA to be launched from London around the world. Regarding relations with EU member states, London should treat these old and important trading partners as they would any other countries.

Specifically, as a number of European states will qualify for the proposed GFTA they must be told flatly that they are welcome to also abandon the suffocating strictures of a sclerotic, deflationary, economically comatose Europe if they so choose, or remain enchained by the only continent in the world presently with negligible rates of growth. Assuming they qualify, these European states will always be welcome, but leaving the EU and embarking on another course is a choice they must make – as the UK will have just done – and a matter for their democracies.

The Global Free-Trade Alliance (GFTA)

As is presently true about British thinking regarding the UK's place in the new era, the world's free-trade agenda is also in a rut. While battle swirls over whether the UK should stay in or leave the

EU, debate almost never centres on the real-world consequences of what should come next. Without drawing up an alternative geoeconomic and geopolitical strategy for the country, it is almost impossible to have a proper grown-up discussion of what ought to happen should the UK vote to leave Brussels in 2017.

Perhaps the worst policy outcome would be to vote to leave, without planning in great detail what ought to immediately follow such an historic decision. Personally, I'm inclined to favour the UK going its own way, but only with such a plan in place. The GFTA provides such a way forward, a concrete map for reaching Drake's stars. The GFTA is based on work I began for the Heritage Foundation in Washington over a decade ago, that made its way to these shores in a monograph for the IEA early in the 2000s (Hulsman 2001a).

Likewise, the world's free-trade agenda has been utterly neutered. Six years back the Doha WTO global free-trade round collapsed. Just recently attempts to revive a portion of the broader agenda – focusing efforts on streamlining border control bureaucracies – came to nothing as it was blocked by India. Multilateralism has now failed empirically for 13 years.

At this point it is glaringly obvious we simply cannot get 160-plus countries to agree to favour the common flavour of an ice cream cone, let alone the more momentous changes necessary to facilitate global free trade. Plurilateral agreements – coalitions of the willing making deals among themselves – have emerged as the last, best chance for further global trade liberalisation. As I noted a decade ago (2004), the UK government's mantra must be 'Free Trade By Any Means' (Feulner et al. 2004). And indeed, the GFTA is designed to complement, rather than replace, other multilateral and bilateral UK trading initiatives.

Breaking the Gordian knot surrounding both these major policy problems revolves around convincing the government – should the UK vote to leave the EU – to immediately then put forward a British proposal for a Global Free-Trade Association

(GFTA). The GFTA would be a rules-based organisation. To qualify, countries would meet numerical conditions relating to four main criteria regarding: a country's open trading policies, transparent and open foreign investment policies and capital flows, minimal regulations designed not to impede business and trade, and secure property rights.

To qualify, these numerical conditions would have to be met ahead of a country joining. The GFTA thus awards nations for their genuine, proven commitment to economic freedom. GFTA membership would be based on an objective analysis of a country's commitment to free trade in goods, services and investment, using the Index of Economic Freedom's assessment as the determining authority (Miles et al. 2004).[1]

In 2004, the Index ranked countries on a scale of 1–5, with 1 being the score of the most economically free countries and 5 amounting to the least free. Using the Index, countries receiving a score of 1 or 2 in each of the four categories qualified for the GFTA. Initially, 12 countries qualified, while tantalisingly a further 19 states – representing every region of the globe – qualified in three of the four categories. With small domestic (and beneficial) liberalising reforms in place, this second cohort could quickly have joined the GFTA, should they have chosen to do so.

To be clear, GFTA would not amount to a treaty. Instead, it would be a parliament-inspired initiative offering free trade and market access to the UK (and all other global GFTA members) with the lowest possible barriers. Parliament would authorise that GFTA members would have unfettered access to the UK market – with no tariffs, quotas or other trade barriers – on the single condition that they reciprocate this access to their own markets.

As the years pass, and GFTA proves its magnetic attraction as its membership grows increasingly prosperous, as standing

---

1   At the time we looked at other freedom indices and found strikingly similar results in terms of membership.

legislation, admitting new members who meet the criteria would not require any additional parliamentary vote. On the other hand, parliamentary legislation should include an enforcement mechanism rescinding special access to British markets if another GFTA member imposes undue trade barriers against British goods and services or if a member enacts policies that cause it to fall short of the numerical qualifying criteria, which are re-evaluated every year.[2] When they join, GFTA member states must agree to the stipulation that if they fail to meet the numerical targets in the future, they will have a one-year grace period to correct the lapse, or they will be automatically ejected from the association.

Nor will such a novel and creative trading initiative run foul of existing multilateral treaties. GFTA is certainly in line with Article 24 of the General Agreement on Tariffs and Trade (GATT), meeting the requirement that 'A regional arrangement must facilitate trade among its members, and not raise trade barriers between its members and other nations' (Miles et al. 2004).

Also, GFTA does not run foul of American law, a vital consideration given that the US and the UK were by far the largest and most intertwined economies then qualifying for GFTA membership.[3] American Most Favoured Nation (MFN) standards are not breached, as the numerical criteria mean that all countries are treated the same. There can be no legal objections to the GFTA; joining is strictly an economic and political decision.

GFTA criteria in detail

The four qualifying criteria for GFTA membership eligibility can be delineated in more detail (see Miles et al. 2004). In terms of

---

2 A decade ago, we found strikingly little change in the year-to-year qualifying membership for GFTA; my 2014 update has confirmed this initial finding.

3 In 2013, the US accounted for fully 27 per cent of all British Foreign Direct Investment, easily amounting to the largest single source (see Spickerwell 2013).

trade policy, countries are deemed freer if they have minimal barriers to trade, including low tariffs, and minimal import licenses, controls, quotas and other non-tariff barriers. To attain GFTA membership, the average tariff rate should be no higher than 9 per cent (Hulsman and Schavey 2001).

Regarding capital flows and foreign investment, countries score higher if they possess an open investment regime, including a transparent and open investment code, impartial domestic treatment of foreign investment and an efficient and speedy approval process.

The Index's Property Rights score is based on the bedrock notion that a central tenet for the exchange of goods and services is an established rule of law – endorsed by an independent, fair and efficient judicial system – that protects private property and provides an environment in which business transactions take place with a high degree of certainty.

The Regulatory score is based on the idea that a country with a significant degree of economic freedom must not impose an undue regulatory burden on entrepreneurs or businesses. Key elements include an efficient, transparent licensing system that allows a business to be established quickly, and allows for an equitable application of regulations. Regulation must not significantly increase the cost of doing business.

In the analysis based on the 2004 Index – which is updated below – an above-average score (a 1 or a 2 out of 5) was necessary in each category for a country to be eligible for GFTA membership. In other words, these are truly the nations of the world that in policy terms are committed to free trade in goods, services and investment. The GFTA is a coalition of the willing, an alliance of genuine free-trading states who, believing free trade is central to their country's continuing prosperity, wish to move forward with as many like-minded countries as it is possible to muster.

Initial GFTA membership and the updated cohort

In the initial assessment, 11 countries qualified outright for GFTA membership, with a further 20 within immediate sight. The geographic range of this putative membership truly spanned the globe. Australia, Iceland, New Zealand, Singapore, the UK and the US all made the grade, along with EU members Denmark, Estonia, Finland, Ireland and Luxembourg. The qualifiers roughly amounted to the Anglosphere plus the free-trading European periphery.

As I noted in a speech in 2004, 'It is no accident that the freest economies in the world have generally adopted the Anglo-Saxon capitalist model of growth. According to Heritage's 2001 Index of Economic Freedom, 7 of the 10 most free global economies are former colonies of an eighth, the UK (Bahrain, the US, Australia, New Zealand, Hong Kong (counted separately from China), Singapore, Ireland' (Hulsman 2004)). Given their similar organic histories, it is unsurprising that a congruent politico-economic culture has naturally grown out of these like circumstances.

However, the GFTA is about far more than the Anglosphere, which at its most deterministic amounts to a fevered reactionary dream that somehow the rest of the world will acquiesce to the re-establishment of the British Empire. While there is little doubt that the Empire laid the very real seeds for the common, modern, economic success of some of its former components, GFTA is – above everything else – an inclusive organisation, which is agnostic as to how its membership imbibed free-trade principles; rather it focuses on the concrete reality that its members have 'walked the walk,' and are committed proponents of free trade as the route to prosperity.

As for the tier of European states that qualify, obviously they have a choice to make, one that is likely to grow dicier by the year. As it becomes apparent to all but its most gormless cheerleaders that the EU simply is not recovering and growing in any sort of meaningful way, the temptation of joining up with a dynamic GFTA just next door will become ever harder to ignore. Even now, it is the UK and the US that are the only major G7 states truly bouncing back from the Great Recession. Given corporatist policies in becalmed Germany, wilfully blind France and calamitous Italy, it is only a matter of time before the European qualifiers for the GFTA cast about for alternatives. The GFTA will be already at hand.

It is easy, but misguided, to be sniffy about the fact that relatively few countries initially qualified for the GFTA, and that of the original list only the US and the UK were large economic players on the global stage. This is wrongheaded in two respects. First, the combined GDP of the initial 12 accounted in 2001 for more than one third of global GDP (37 per cent), proving of marginally greater heft than EU global market share (29 per cent), or even NAFTA (33 per cent). Even in its initial stages, the GFTA would be more than economically robust enough to provide the UK with a viable strategic and economic option (Hulsman 2001b). It is hard to think of a better siren song drawing others to this British-inspired grouping than full access on the best possible terms to this massive combined market.

The countries on the edge of eligibility would transform this already formidable alliance into a truly global movement. Bahrain (trade reforms needed), Canada (foreign investment reform), Chile (regulation reform), Switzerland (regulation), Botswana (trade policy), El Salvador (property rights reform), Israel (regulation), Trinidad and Tobago (regulation) and Uruguay are all knocking on the door, representing countries – in true Drakean fashion – from every corner of the world. As Baroness Thatcher noted about the GFTA concept, 'Not only would this arrangement work to stimulate the members' prosperity: it would act also as a beacon and an example to others' (Thatcher 2002: 405).

Likewise, core EU countries are in many cases only one notch away from joining, even if that impediment – a change in attitude to regulation – is unlikely to be overcome for a generation. Nevertheless, as things in the EU worsen, the door to GFTA membership must be left open. France, Italy, Portugal and Spain may not be likely to change their ways for 20 years. But, indeed, GFTA is about never saying never to prospective partners who eventually may well see the error of their protectionist ways.

In updating these initial striking numbers, it is gratifying to see both the continuity of that initial membership (Anglosphere plus European periphery) and that the cohort has expanded to make the potential GFTA a truly global alternative for the UK.[4] The Index numbers are now calculated on a 0–100 scale, but the subheadings of Property Rights, Investment Freedom and Trade Freedom remain, as does Regulatory Efficiency, which is derived by looking at the subheadings of Business Freedom, Labour Freedom, and Monetary Freedom. Using 70 out of 100 as the base score needed in each category for GFTA entry, and again saying that a country missing out on only one of these benchmarks stands on the cusp of membership, we are able to cleanly update the results.

Again, nearly every country in the initial 2004 class still qualifies (10 of the original 11 candidates): the UK, the US, Singapore, Australia, New Zealand, Ireland, Denmark, Estonia, Finland and Iceland. In addition, Anglosphere-oriented Canada now makes the grade. But a further list of European states could also be members if they so chose: Switzerland, Sweden, the Netherlands, Germany, Austria, the Czech Republic, Norway and Belgium.

Even better, the candidate list has a far more global flavour now, with Chile and Uruguay representing South America, economic heavyweights Japan, Taiwan and South Korea from Asia, Botswana from Africa, and Israel from the Middle East. There is little doubt that the 26 members of the 2014 qualifying class are big enough in terms of economic heft to be an incredibly attractive magnetic draw to future members.

---

4   For the basis to these updated numbers, see Miller et al. (2014).

The list of countries just one criterion removed from GFTA membership is equally impressive. Globally, property rights tends to be the area most in need of liberalisation, with Mauritius, Bahrain, Lithuania, Georgia, Columbia, Jordan, Armenia, Latvia, Peru, Poland, Hungary, Mexico, Jamaica, Romania, Dominica and Slovenia all needing to undertake reforms here. Regulatory sclerosis stops France, Portugal, Malta, Spain and Luxembourg from qualifying, while a lack of investment freedom stymies Qatar, St Lucia and Cyprus. However, a concerted liberalising effort would find these further 24 countries able to join the GFTA in relatively short order.

The GFTA will not morph into yet another top-heavy international organisation. Rather than having a standing secretariat, disappearing into the alphabet soup of ineffectual international organisations, the GFTA will merely amount to a formalised meeting of member states' trade ministers, staffs and technical experts. Any specific technical working group would exist for only as long as its specific task was being addressed (i.e. common accounting standards).

Further collective decisions on trade initiatives would be made on a consensual basis, such as codifying uniform standards on capital flows, subsidies and regulation, to further minimise barriers within the alliance. The overall direction of GFTA initiatives will allow for the freeing up of capital within the alliance, as well as diminishing all hidden tariffs impeding trade between its members.

The advantages of living in Drake's world

The advantages to this dynamic, creative new initiative are legion. First, the whole GFTA process would require minimal negotiation, as membership is solely decided using a rules-based, numerical system, basing itself on a country's existing policies, rather than endless negotiations revolving around 'concessions'.

As such, the establishment of the GFTA would happen far faster than other existing trading options – no further parliamentary approval would be needed to admit new GFTA members down the road, allowing them the immediate privileges of membership.

Second, sovereignty is unaffected by GFTA membership (utterly unlike the EU). Individual countries can violate the GFTA membership requirements at any time – but this of course will cost them privileged access to the other GFTA members' domestic markets. As the GFTA amounts to a coalition of the virtuous, as its members must qualify to join, they need undertake no major internal policy changes to benefit, but merely keep doing what they are already doing. As its membership is, by definition, like-minded about the overall benefits of free trade, GFTA members ought to be able to quickly agree on further free-trade initiatives between its member states.

Third, the GFTA amounts to a carrot-based approach. As its membership grows, the GFTA will become ever-increasingly attractive, providing the impetus for a worldwide virtuous cycle of countries opening their markets in order to gain GFTA access. There will be a tipping point here, with GFTA market access cajoling non-member countries, giving them an incentive to make market-friendly reforms in order to qualify, based on following their own national interests.

Fourth, the GFTA is entirely inclusive, global and voluntary: membership is based solely on a country's demonstrated commitment to a liberal trading order. British sovereignty – so recently wrested away from Brussels – is entirely preserved. The creaking, present series of major trading regimes, from the EU to NAFTA (still wrongly viewed as politically toxic in the US), are based on the age of the sailing ship; that is, on geography, rather than ideology.

Rather, the GFTA is the future, with its commitment to a true economic alliance of like-minded countries from every corner of the globe. As I observed in 2004, 'In the new era the concept of location has been transformed as a result of the telecommunications revolution that is such a salient characteristic of the age of globalisation. To some extent, the Internet has epitomised this death of distance' (Hulsman 2004). Common policies – and not the accident of geography – are what drives the GFTA.

Fifth, in terms of both geopolitics and geoeconomics, the GFTA indelibly enhances the UK's global position. The GFTA countries – with their shared and deep commitment to open and free economies – share similar beliefs as well as market institutions. It is clear to the eye that the truism holds that the GFTA's membership list reads like a 'Who's Who' of British global partners: all of these countries are already allies of the UK, with many of them being part of the common Anglosphere tradition. By creatively and radically further tying the economies of these friends to that of the UK, London has not just made for itself a new economic destiny. It has also underwritten its new geostrategic place in the world.

Importantly, the global aspect of the GFTA allows the UK to establish an enduring link with the rest of the growing world, while hedging its exposure to an utterly sclerotic and growth-deprived Europe.

Sixth, the establishment of the GFTA will ideationally change the very way people and countries think about free trade. Instead of being seen as an unpopular concession, free trade will over time come to be seen for what it is – a policy that gives countries that embrace it a massive economic advantage. In the current dusty tomes of true believers, it is a commonplace to note free trade's obvious economic benefits, a policy that increases a country's productivity, lowers costs and bolsters living standards. For example, Klein et al. (2003) matter-of-factly note that the fundamental benefits of trade outweigh its costs by 100 per cent, or 2-to-1.

But beyond a segment of the academy, such truisms are not the norm. The GFTA will function as a practical experiment, illustrating beyond doubt the relative benefits of open markets and free trade to the wider world. As its members prosper – certainly relative to a moribund EU – the academic arguments will become real to a much wider audience, creating a far more robust pro-free-trade constituency. The GFTA demonstration effect has the power to do nothing less than change the way the world thinks about open markets.

Conclusion: deciphering the riddle of Drake's prayer

At its core, Drake's prayer, though written half a millennium ago, remains true: it is vital in life not to confuse caution and wisdom. Given the present mood in the UK, the likely outcome of any policy following a 'No' vote in an EU referendum will be to do as little as possible, muddling along as close to the shore as can be managed.

That would amount to a dreadful intellectual and policy mistake. For in the GFTA alternative, the UK can truly remake the world it finds itself in, and on its terms. All it takes is a little courage, a little boldness, and the bravery to leave the land – the old ways of doing things – in order to see the stars of a generation of prosperity.

References

Feulner, E. J., Hulsman, J. C. and Schaefer, B. D. (2004) Free trade by any means: how the Global Free Trade Alliance enhances America's overall trading strategy. Heritage Backgrounder 1786, 10 August.

Hulsman, J. C. (2001a) *The World Turned Rightside Up: A New Trading Agenda for the Age of Globalisation*. London: Institute of Economic Affairs.

Hulsman, J. C. (2001b) European disunion: continental anxiety grows as EU tries to punish success. *Investor's Business Daily*, 10 May.

Hulsman, J. C. and Schavey, A. (2001) The Global Free Trade Association: a new trade agenda. Heritage Backgrounder 1441, 16 May.

Hulsman, J. C. (2004) The Global Free Trade Association: preserving and expanding the special relationship in the 21st century. Speech given to the Bruges Group, London, 8 September 2004.

Klein, M. W., Schuh, S. and Triest, R. K. (2003) *Job Creation, Job Destruction, and International Competition*. Kalamazoo, MI: W. E. Upjohn Institute for Employment Research.

Miles, M. A., Feulner, E. J. and O'Grady, M. A. (2004) *2004 Index of Economic Freedom*. Washington, D.C.: The Heritage Foundation and Dow Jones and Company.

Miller, T., Kim, A. B. and Holmes, K. R. (2014) *2014 Index of Economic Freedom*. Washington, D.C.: The Heritage Foundation and Dow Jones and Company.

Spickerwell, S. (2014) In 2013 UK received the most FDI in Europe, and second most in the world after the US. *City AM*, 26 October 2014.

Thatcher, M. (2002) *Statecraft*. London: HarperCollins.

ABOUT THE IEA

The Institute is a research and educational charity (No. CC 235 351), limited by guarantee. Its mission is to improve understanding of the fundamental institutions of a free society by analysing and expounding the role of markets in solving economic and social problems.

The IEA achieves its mission by:

- a high-quality publishing programme
- conferences, seminars, lectures and other events
- outreach to school and college students
- brokering media introductions and appearances

The IEA, which was established in 1955 by the late Sir Antony Fisher, is an educational charity, not a political organisation. It is independent of any political party or group and does not carry on activities intended to affect support for any political party or candidate in any election or referendum, or at any other time. It is financed by sales of publications, conference fees and voluntary donations.

In addition to its main series of publications the IEA also publishes a quarterly journal, *Economic Affairs*.

The IEA is aided in its work by a distinguished international Academic Advisory Council and an eminent panel of Honorary Fellows. Together with other academics, they review prospective IEA publications, their comments being passed on anonymously to authors. All IEA papers are therefore subject to the same rigorous independent refereeing process as used by leading academic journals.

IEA publications enjoy widespread classroom use and course adoptions in schools and universities. They are also sold throughout the world and often translated/reprinted.

Since 1974 the IEA has helped to create a worldwide network of 100 similar institutions in over 70 countries. They are all independent but share the IEA's mission.

Views expressed in the IEA's publications are those of the authors, not those of the Institute (which has no corporate view), its Managing Trustees, Academic Advisory Council members or senior staff.

Members of the Institute's Academic Advisory Council, Honorary Fellows, Trustees and Staff are listed on the following page.

The Institute gratefully acknowledges financial support for its publications programme and other work from a generous benefaction by the late Professor Ronald Coase.

The Institute of Economic Affairs
2 Lord North Street, Westminster, London SW1P 3LB
Tel: 020 7799 8900
Fax: 020 7799 2137
Email: iea@iea.org.uk
Internet: iea.org.uk

Institute of
Economic Affairs

The Future of the Commons – Beyond Market Failure and Government Regulation
Elinor Ostrom et al.
Occasional Paper 148; ISBN 978-0-255-36653-3; £10.00

Redefining the Poverty Debate – Why a War on Markets Is No Substitute for a War on Poverty
Kristian Niemietz
Research Monograph 67; ISBN 978-0-255-36652-6; £12.50

The Euro – the Beginning, the Middle … and the End?
Edited by Philip Booth
Hobart Paperback 39; ISBN 978-0-255-36680-9; £12.50

The Shadow Economy
Friedrich Schneider & Colin C. Williams
Hobart Paper 172; ISBN 978-0-255-36674-8; £12.50

Quack Policy – Abusing Science in the Cause of Paternalism
Jamie Whyte
Hobart Paper 173; ISBN 978-0-255-36673-1; £10.00

Foundations of a Free Society
Eamonn Butler
Occasional Paper 149; ISBN 978-0-255-36687-8; £12.50

The Government Debt Iceberg
Jagadeesh Gokhale
Research Monograph 68; ISBN 978-0-255-36666-3; £10.00

A U-Turn on the Road to Serfdom
Grover Norquist
Occasional Paper 150; ISBN 978-0-255-36686-1; £10.00

New Private Monies – A Bit-Part Player?
Kevin Dowd
Hobart Paper 174; ISBN 978-0-255-36694-6; £10.00

From Crisis to Confidence – Macroeconomics after the Crash
Roger Koppl
Hobart Paper 175; ISBN 978-0-255-36693-9; £12.50

Advertising in a Free Society
Ralph Harris and Arthur Seldon
With an introduction by Christopher Snowdon
Hobart Paper 176; ISBN 978-0-255-36696-0; £12.50

Selfishness, Greed and Capitalism: Debunking Myths about the Free Market
Christopher Snowdon
Hobart Paper 177; ISBN 978-0-255-36677-9; £12.50

Waging the War of Ideas
John Blundell
Occasional Paper 131; ISBN 978-0-255-36684-7; £12.50

Other IEA publications

Comprehensive information on other publications and the wider work of the IEA can be found at www.iea.org.uk. To order any publication please see below.

Personal customers

Orders from personal customers should be directed to the IEA:

Clare Rusbridge
IEA
2 Lord North Street
FREEPOST LON10168
London SW1P 3YZ
Tel: 020 7799 8907. Fax: 020 7799 2137
Email: sales@iea.org.uk

Trade customers

All orders from the book trade should be directed to the IEA's distributor:

NBN International (IEA Orders)
Orders Dept.
NBN International
10 Thornbury Road
Plymouth PL6 7PP
Tel: 01752 202301, Fax: 01752 202333
Email: orders@nbninternational.com

IEA subscriptions

The IEA also offers a subscription service to its publications. For a single annual payment (currently £42.00 in the UK), subscribers receive every monograph the IEA publishes. For more information please contact:

Clare Rusbridge
Subscriptions
IEA
2 Lord North Street
FREEPOST LON10168
London SW1P 3YZ
Tel: 020 7799 8907, Fax: 020 7799 2137
Email: crusbridge@iea.org.uk